SAMS
Teach Yourself

CSS

Russ Weakley

800 East 96th Street, Indianapolis, Indiana 46240 USA

Sams Teach Yourself CSS in 10 Minutes

Copyright © 2006 by Sams Publishing

International Standard Book Number: 0-672-32745-7

Library of Congress Catalog Card Number: 2004097471

Printed in the United States of America

Fifth printing: February 2008

10   09   08   8   7   6   5

Trademarks

Warning and Disclaimer

Bulk Sales

Sams Publishing offers excellent discounts on this book when ordered in quantity for bulk purchases or special sales. For more information, please contact

U.S. Corporate and Government Sales
1-800-382-3419
corpsales@pearsontechgroup.com

For sales outside of the U.S., please contact

International Sales
international@pearsoned.com

SENIOR ACQUISITIONS EDITOR
Linda Bump Harrison

DEVELOPMENT EDITOR
Jon Steever

MANAGING EDITOR
Charlotte Clapp

PROJECT EDITOR
Mandie Frank

COPY EDITOR
Jessica McCarty

INDEXER
Aaron Black

PROOFREADER
Brad Engels

TECHNICAL EDITOR
Kevin Ruse

PUBLISHING COORDINATOR
Vanessa Evans

MULTIMEDIA DEVELOPER
Dan Scherf

DESIGNER
Gary Adair

PAGE LAYOUT
Nonie Ratcliff

Table of Contents

About the Author

Russ Weakley has worked in the design field for more than 18 years. During the last nine years, he has focused on web design through his own business, Max Design. He is also the web designer for the Australian Museum.

He co-chairs the Web Standards Group with Peter Firminger. The role of this group is to assist web developers in learning about new technologies and accessibility issues. He also co-founded Web Essentials, which organizes web development conferences and workshops that attract speakers and delegates from all over the world.

Internationally recognized for his presentations and workshops on web development, standards, and accessibility, Weakley has also produced a series of widely acclaimed CSS-based tutorials including Listamatic, Listamatic2, Listutorial, Floatutorial, and Selectutorial, which can all be found on his website at http://www.maxdesign.com.au.

Acknowledgments

Thanks to the Sams team, in particular Linda Harrison, for giving me the opportunity to write this book.

Thanks to everyone who has given me comments, criticism, and positive feedback on my online tutorials. This feedback has given me confidence and insight into the problems other designers and developers face when learning CSS.

Thanks to Lisa Miller, who willingly proofread and user-tested every lesson.

Finally, thanks to my partner, Anna, for her patience, support, and encouragement throughout the writing of this book.

We Want to Hear from You!

As the reader of this book, *you* are our most important critic and commentator. We value your opinion and want to know what we're doing right, what we could do better, what areas you'd like to see us publish in, and any other words of wisdom you're willing to pass our way.

You can email or write me directly to let me know what you did or didn't like about this book—as well as what we can do to make our books stronger.

Please note that I cannot help you with technical problems related to the topic of this book, and that due to the high volume of mail I receive, I might not be able to reply to every message.

When you write, please be sure to include this book's title and author as well as your name and phone or email address. I will carefully review your comments and share them with the author and editors who worked on the book.

Email: webdev@samspublishing.com

Mail: Mark Taber
          Associate Publisher
          Sams Publishing
          800 East 96th Street
          Indianapolis, IN 46240 USA

Reader Services

For more information about this book or another Sams Publishing title, visit our website at www.samspublishing.com. Type the ISBN (excluding hyphens) or the title of a book in the Search field to find the page you're looking for.

Introduction

Cascading Style Sheets (CSS) is a simple and powerful language for adding style to web documents. Whether you are a web designer, developer, or anywhere in between, CSS is an important part of developing websites.

Many web developers still use tables for layout and do not understand the benefits of CSS. Although there are many good CSS resources and books available, people are often overwhelmed by the sheer volume of information. It is hard to decide the best place to start.

Sams Teach Yourself CSS in 10 Minutes is designed to help you get a handle on CSS quickly and easily through a series of step-by-step lessons.

Who Is This Book For?

This book is for you if any (or all) of the following apply:

- You're new to CSS

- You want a simple, hands-on guide to using CSS

- You want to quickly learn how to get the most out of CSS

- You want to learn new ways to use CSS

How This Book Works

Sams Teach Yourself CSS in 10 Minutes is divided into 22 lessons that gradually build on one another. By the end of the book, you should have a solid understanding of CSS and how to apply it in a variety of real-world situations.

Each lesson is written in simple steps so that you can quickly grasp the overall concept and put it into practice. The lessons are also designed to stand alone so that you can jump directly to particular topics as needed.

Online Support Files

Each lesson from *Sams Teach Yourself CSS in 10 Minutes* has support files that can be downloaded from the Sams Publishing website. The files can either be downloaded as a single file for all lessons, or individually for each lesson.

The address is http://www.samspublishing.com/.

Conventions Used in This Book

This book uses different typefaces to differentiate between HTML/CSS code and other content.

HTML and CSS code are presented using monospace type. Bold text indicates a change in code from the previous step.

 Note A Note presents pertinent pieces of information related to the surrounding discussion.

 Caution A Caution advises you about potential problems having to do with CSS or its implementation in specific browsers.

 Tip Tip offers advice or demonstrates an easier way to do something.

Lesson 1
Understanding CSS

In this lesson, you will learn about Cascading Style Sheets and why you should use them.

What Is CSS?

Cascading Style Sheets (CSS) is a language that works with HTML documents to define the way content is presented. The presentation is specified with *styles* that are placed directly into HTML elements, the head of the HTML document, or separate style sheets.

Style sheets contain a number of CSS rules. Each rule selects elements in an HTML document. These rules then define how the elements will be styled.

Any number of HTML files can be linked to a single CSS file.

What Does Cascading Mean?

There are three types of style sheets that can influence the presentation of an HTML document in a browser. These are

- **Browser style sheets**—Browsers apply style sheets to all web documents. Although these style sheets vary from browser to browser, they all have common characteristics, including black text, blue links, and purple visited links. These are referred to as *default* browser style sheets.

- **User style sheets**—A user is anyone who looks at your website. Most modern browsers allow users to set their own style sheets within their browser. These style sheets will override the browser's default style sheets—for that user only.

- **Author style sheets**—The author is the person who develops the website—you! As soon as you apply a basic style sheet to a page, you have added an author style sheet. Author styles generally override user styles, which override browser styles. The cascade is shown in Figure 1.1.

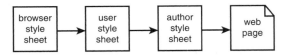

FIGURE 1.1 The three types of style sheets that influence the presentation of a web page.

Cascading means that styles can fall (or cascade) from one style sheet to another. The cascade is used to determine which rules will take precedence and be applied to a document.

For example, rules in author style sheets will generally take precedence over rules in user style sheets. Rules in user and author style sheets will take precedence over rules in the browser's default style sheet.

Where Does CSS Come From? CSS is a recommendation of the *World Wide Web Consortium (W3C)*. The W3C is an industry consortium of web stakeholders including universities; companies such as Microsoft, Netscape, and Macromedia; and experts in web-related fields.

One of the W3C's roles is to produce recommendations for a range of aspects of the Web. CSS1 became a recommendation in late 1996, CSS2 became a recommendation in May 1998, and CSS2.1 became a recommendation in January 2003.

Why Use CSS?

Some of the benefits of using CSS for authors include

- **Easy to maintain**—The power of CSS is that a single CSS file can be used to control the appearance of multiple HTML documents. Changing the appearance of an entire site can be done by editing one CSS file rather than multiple HTML documents.

- **Smaller file sizes**—CSS allows authors to remove all presentation from HTML documents, including layout tables, spacer images, decorative images, fonts, colors, widths, heights, and background images. Presentation can then be controlled by CSS files. This can dramatically reduce the file sizes of HTML documents.

- **Increased accessibility**—CSS, combined with well-structured HTML documents, can aid devices such as screen readers. With presentational markup removed, the only thing that a screen reader encounters is structural content. CSS also can be used to increase the clickable area of links, as well as control line height and text line lengths for users with motor skill or cognitive difficulties.

- **Different media**—CSS can be styled specifically for different media, including browsers, printers, handheld devices, and projectors—without changing the content or document structure in any way.

- **More control over typography**—CSS allows authors to control the presentation of content with properties such as `capitalize`, `uppercase`, `lowercase`, `text-decoration`, `letter-spacing`, `word-spacing`, `text-indent`, and `line-height`. CSS can also be used to add margins, borders, padding, background color, and background images to any HTML element.

Summary

In this lesson, you learned about Cascading Style Sheets and why you should use them. You also learned where style sheets come from and the three types of style sheets that can affect a web page.

LESSON 2
Using CSS Rules

In this lesson, you will learn the syntax and rules of the Cascading Style Sheet (CSS) language. You will learn the components of CSS rules, including selectors, declarations, properties, and values. You will learn how to style a series of simple HTML elements. You will also learn how to use shorthand properties.

Setting Up the HTML Code

The HTML code for this lesson will be comprised of three elements—
<h1>, <h2>, and <p>, as shown in Listing 2.1.

LISTING 2.1 HTML Code Containing the Markup for Lesson 2

```
<h1>
    Level 1 heading
</h1>
<h2>
    Level 2 heading
</h2>
<p>
    Lorem ipsum dolor sit amet, consectetuer...
</p>
```

Creating a Rule Set

A *rule*, or *rule set*, is a statement that tells browsers how to render particular elements on an HTML page. A rule set consists of a selector followed by a declaration block. Inside the declaration block, there can be one or more declarations. Each declaration contains a property and a value as shown in Figure 2.1.

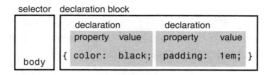

FIGURE 2.1 Diagram of rule set structure.

The first step in creating a rule set is to decide on a *selector*. The selector "selects" the elements on an HTML page that are affected by the rule set. The selector consists of everything up to (but not including) the first left curly bracket. The selectors used in this lesson are shown in Listing 2.2. Selectors are discussed in more detail in Lesson 3, "Selectors in Action."

LISTING 2.2   CSS Code Showing Selectors

```
h1
h2
p
```

Next, the *declaration block* must be created. A declaration block is a container that consists of everything between (and including) the curly brackets. The declaration blocks used in this lesson are highlighted in Listing 2.3.

LISTING 2.3   CSS Code Showing Declaration Blocks

```
h1 {...}
h2 {...}
p {...}
```

Inside the declaration block, there are one or more declarations. *Declarations* tell a browser how to draw any element on a page that is selected. A declaration consists of a property and one or more values, separated by a colon. The end of each declaration is indicated with a semicolon.

The declarations used in this lesson are highlighted in Listing 2.4.

LISTING 2.4   CSS Code Showing Declarations

```
h1 { text-align: center; }
h2 { font-style: italic; }
p { color: maroon; }
```

Using Whitespace   Whitespace (spaces, tabs, line feeds, and carriage returns) is allowed around rule sets, as well as inside declaration blocks.

Rule sets can be laid out to suit your needs. Some developers prefer all declarations within a single line to conserve space as shown in Listing 2.5. Others prefer to place each declaration on a new line to make the rule sets easier to read as shown in Listing 2.6.

LISTING 2.5   CSS Code Showing Single-Line Rule Set

```
h2 { font-style: italic; text-align: center; color: navy; }
```

LISTING 2.6   CSS Code Showing Multiple-Line Rule Set

```
h2
{
    font-style: italic;
    text-align: center;
    color: navy;
}
```

The *property* is an aspect of the element that you are choosing to style. There can be only one property within each declaration unless a shorthand property is used (see "Using Shorthand Properties," later in this lesson). The properties used in this lesson are highlighted in bold in Listing 2.7.

LISTING 2.7   CSS Code Showing Properties

```
h1 { text-align: center; }
h2 { font-style: italic; }
p { color: maroon; }
```

The *value* is the exact style you want to set for the property. Values can include length, percentage, color, url, keyword, and shape. The values used in this lesson are highlighted (in bold) in Listing 2.8.

LISTING 2.8   CSS Code Showing Values

```
h1 { text-align: center; }
h2 { font-style: italic; }
p { color: maroon; }
```

The first rule set will target the <h1> element and align it in the center of the browser window.

The second rule set will target the <h2> element and render it in italics.

The third selector will target the <p> element and color all the text inside the element maroon.

The results of this styling applied to the HTML code in Listing 2.1 are shown in Figure 2.2.

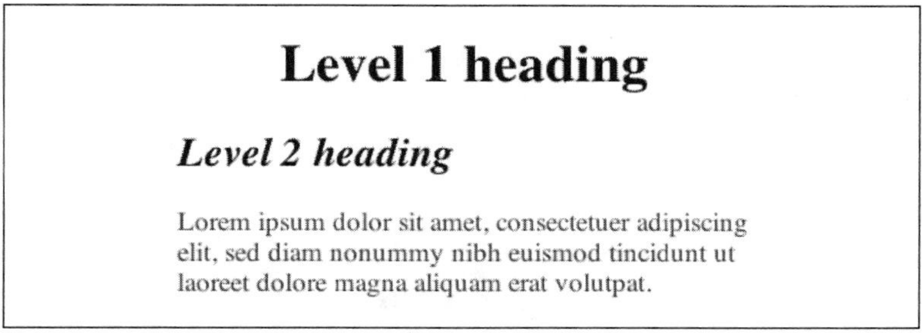

Level 1 heading

Level 2 heading

Lorem ipsum dolor sit amet, consectetuer adipiscing elit, sed diam nonummy nibh euismod tincidunt ut laoreet dolore magna aliquam erat volutpat.

FIGURE 2.2   Screenshot of styled elements.

Using Multiple Declarations

More than one declaration can be used within a declaration block. Each declaration must be separated with a semicolon.

In this example, the <h1> and <h2> elements will be styled with a new declaration—color: navy;. The <h2> element also will be styled with text-align: center;, which will align it in the center of the browser window. The new declarations are highlighted in Listing 2.9. The results are shown in Figure 2.3.

LISTING 2.9   CSS Code Showing Multiple Declarations

```
h1
{
    text-align: center;
    color: navy;
}

h2
{
    font-style: italic;
    text-align: center;
    color: navy;
}

p
{
    color: maroon;
}
```

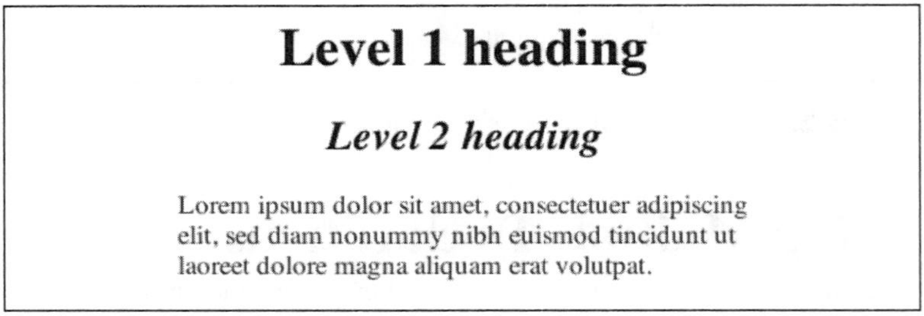

Level 1 heading

Level 2 heading

Lorem ipsum dolor sit amet, consectetuer adipiscing elit, sed diam nonummy nibh euismod tincidunt ut laoreet dolore magna aliquam erat volutpat.

FIGURE 2.3   Screenshot of elements styled with multiple declarations.

Combining Selectors

When several selectors share the same declarations, they may be grouped together to prevent the need to write the same rule more than once. Each selector must be separated by a comma.

The <h1> and <h2> elements share two declarations, so parts of the two rule sets can be combined to be more efficient as shown in Listing 2.10.

LISTING 2.10   CSS Code Showing Combined Selectors

```
h1, h2
{
    text-align: center;
    color: navy;
}

h2
{
    font-style: italic;
}

p
{
    color: maroon;
}
```

 Adding CSS Comments   CSS comments can be added to CSS to explain your code. Like HTML comments, CSS comments will be ignored by the browser. A CSS comment begins with /* and ends with */. Comments can appear before or within rule sets as well as across multiple lines. They also can be used to comment out entire rules or individual declarations.

Using Shorthand Properties

Shorthand properties allow the values of several properties to be specified within a single property. Shorthand properties are easier to write and maintain. They also make CSS files more concise.

For example, the <h2> element can be styled with font-style, font-variant, font-weight, font-size, line-height, and font-family as shown in Listing 2.11, or with a single font property as shown in Listing 2.12 and Figure 2.4.

Most shorthand properties do not require the values to be placed in a set order. However, when using the font property, it is safer to set values in the order specified by the W3C, which is font-style, font-variant, font-weight, font-size, line-height, and font-family.

When font-size and line-height are used within the font property, they must be specified with font-size first, followed by a forward slash (/), followed by line-height, as shown in Listing 2.12.

LISTING 2.11   CSS Code Highlighting All font Properties

```
h1, h2
{
    text-align: center;
    color: navy;
}

h2
{
    font-style: italic;
    font-variant: small-caps;
    font-weight: bold;
    font-size: 100%;
    line-height: 120%;
    font-family: arial, helvetica, sans-serif;
}

p
{
    color: maroon;
}
```

LISTING 2.12   CSS Code Highlighting Shorthand font Property

```
h1, h2
{
    text-align: center;
    color: navy;
}

h2
{
    font: italic small-caps bold 100%/120% arial, helvetica,
sans-serif;
}

p
{
    color: maroon;
}
```

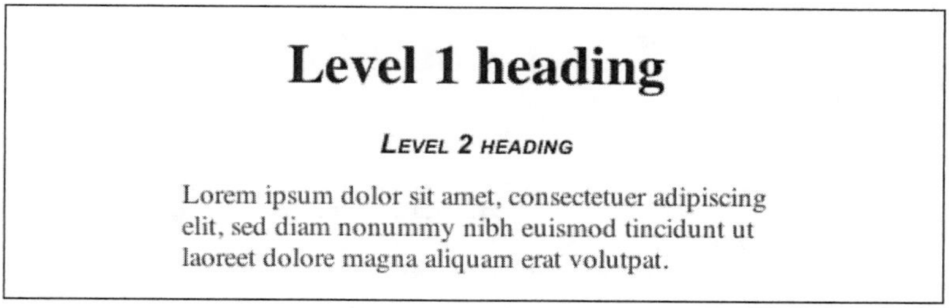

Level 1 heading

LEVEL 2 HEADING

Lorem ipsum dolor sit amet, consectetuer adipiscing
elit, sed diam nonummy nibh euismod tincidunt ut
laoreet dolore magna aliquam erat volutpat.

FIGURE 2.4   Screenshot of styled <h2> element.

Values for the shorthand font property include `font-style`, `font-variant`, `font-weight`, `font-size`, `line-height`, and `font-family`. However, all of these values do not need to be included in a shorthand declaration. For example, for the <p> element, you might want to only specify values for `font-size` and `font-family` as shown in Listing 2.13.

In this case, `font-style`, `font-variant`, `font-weight`, and `line-height` are not included in the shorthand property, so they will be assigned their default value. The results can be seen in Figure 2.5.

LISTING 2.13   CSS Code Highlighting All `font` Properties

```
h1, h2
{
    text-align: center;
    color: navy;
}

h2
{
    font: italic small-caps bold 100%/120% arial, helvetica,
sans-serif;
}

p
{
    color: maroon;
    font: 80% arial, helvetica, sans-serif;
}
```

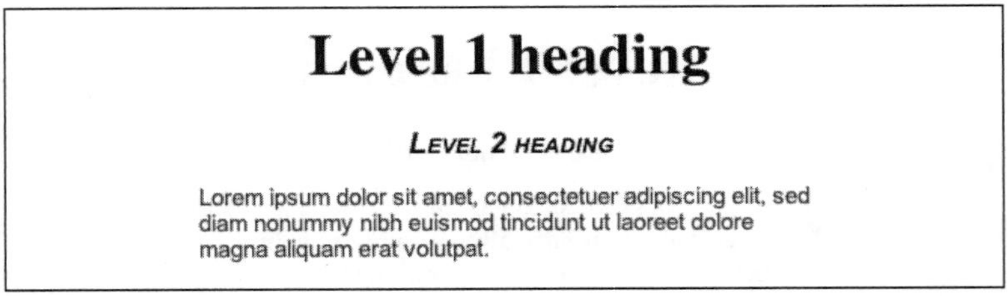

> # Level 1 heading
>
> ## LEVEL 2 HEADING
>
> Lorem ipsum dolor sit amet, consectetuer adipiscing elit, sed diam nonummy nibh euismod tincidunt ut laoreet dolore magna aliquam erat volutpat.

FIGURE 2.5   Screenshot of styled <p> element.

Using Shorthand Borders

Border properties also can be converted to the shorthand border property. The <h1> element can be styled with border-width, border-style, and border-color as shown in Listing 2.14, or with a single border property as shown in Listing 2.15. The results can be seen in Figure 2.6.

LISTING 2.14   CSS Code Highlighting All border Properties

```
h1, h2
{
    text-align: center;
    color: navy;
}

h1
{
    border-width: 1px;
    border-style: solid;
    border-color: gray;
}

h2
{
    font: italic small-caps bold 100%/120% arial, helvetica,
sans-serif;
}
```

continues

```
p
{
    color: maroon;
    font: 80% arial, helvetica, sans-serif;
}
```

LISTING 2.15   CSS Code Highlighting the Shorthand border
Property

```
h1, h2
{
    text-align: center;
    color: navy;
}


h1
{
    border: 1px solid gray;
}


h2
{
    font: italic small-caps bold 100%/120% arial, helvetica,
sans-serif;
}


p
{
    color: maroon;
    font: 80% arial, helvetica, sans-serif;
}
```

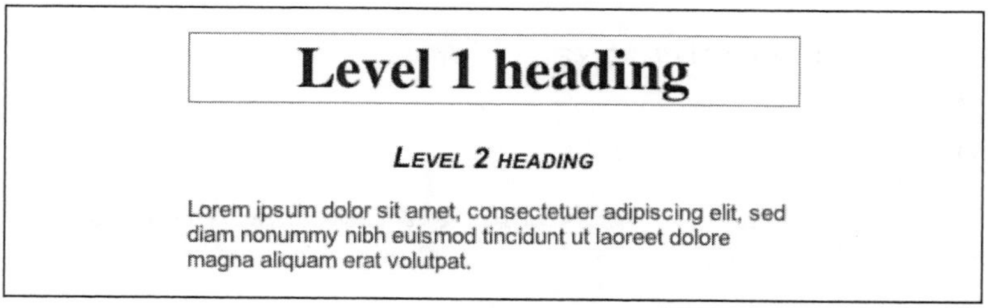

FIGURE 2.6   Screenshot of styled <h1> elements.

Using Shorthand Margins and Padding

Margins create space between the edge of an element and the edge of any adjacent elements. Padding creates the space between the edge of the element and its content (see Lesson 5, "Getting to Know the CSS Box Model," for more information). The margin and padding shorthand properties also can be used to make CSS code more concise.

The margin property can combine margin-top, margin-right, margin-bottom, and margin-left. The padding property can combine padding-top, padding-right, padding-bottom, and padding-left.

The margin and padding properties also can be used to style different values for each side of an element. Values are applied in the following order: top, right, bottom, and left—clockwise, starting at the top.

The <p> element can be styled with padding-top, padding-right, padding-bottom, and padding-left as shown in Listing 2.16, or with a single padding property as shown in Listing 2.17.

LISTING 2.16   CSS Code Highlighting All padding Properties

```
h1, h2
{
    text-align: center;
    color: navy;
}

h1
{
    border: 1px solid gray;
}

h2
{
    font: italic small-caps bold 100%/120% arial, helvetica,
sans-serif;
}

p
{
    color: maroon;
```

continues

```
    font: 80% arial, helvetica, sans-serif;
    padding-top: 1em;
    padding-right: 2em;
    padding-bottom: 3em;
    padding-left: 4em;
}
```

LISTING 2.17   CSS Code Highlighting a Shorthand padding Property

```
h1, h2
{
    text-align: center;
    color: navy;
}

h1
{
    border: 1px solid gray;
}

h2
{
    font: italic small-caps bold 100%/120% arial, helvetica,
sans-serif;
}

p
{
    color: maroon;
    font: 80% arial, helvetica, sans-serif;
    padding: 1em 2em 3em 4em;
}
```

You can use one, two, three, and four values within a shorthand declaration.

The declaration p { padding: 1em; } will apply 1em of padding to all sides of an element.

The declaration p { padding: 1em 2em; } will apply 1em of padding to the top and bottom, and 2em of padding to the left and right of an element.

The declaration p { padding: 1em 2em 3em; } will apply 1em of padding to the top, 2em of padding to the left and right, and 3em to the bottom of an element.

The declaration p { padding: 1em 2em 3em 4em; } will apply 1em of
padding to the top, 2em of padding to the right, 3em of padding to the
bottom, and 4em of padding to the left of an element.

Other Shorthand Properties

The background property combines background-color, background-
image, background-repeat, background-attachment, and background-
position as shown in Listing 2.18.

LISTING 2.18   CSS Code Highlighting a Shorthand
background Property

```
h1, h2
{
    text-align: center;
    color: navy;
}

h1
{
    border: 1px solid gray;
    background: yellow url(tint.jpg) repeat-y 100% 0;
}

h2
{
    font: italic small-caps bold 100%/120% arial, helvetica,
sans-serif;
}

p
{
    color: maroon;
    font: 80% arial, helvetica, sans-serif;
    padding: 1em 2em 3em 4em;
}
```

The list-style property combines list-style-type, list-style-
position, and list-style-image as shown in Listing 2.19.

LISTING 2.19 CSS Code Highlighting a Shorthand `list` Property

```
h1, h2
{
    text-align: center;
    color: navy;
}

h1
{
    border: 1px solid gray;
    background: yellow url(tint.jpg) repeat-y 100% 0;
}

h2
{
    font: italic small-caps bold 100%/120% arial, helvetica,
sans-serif;
}

p
{
    color: maroon;
    font: 80% arial, helvetica, sans-serif;
    padding: 1em 2em 3em 4em;
}
ul
{
    list-style: square inside;
}
```

Summary

In this lesson, you learned how to use selectors, declarations, properties, shorthand properties, and values to style a series of simple HTML elements. In the next lesson, you will learn about the different types of selectors and how to use them.

LESSON 3
Selectors in Action

In this lesson, you will learn about the different types of selectors and how to use them.

Setting Up the HTML Code

Selectors are one of the most important aspects of CSS because they are used to "select" elements on an HTML page so that they can be styled. The HTML code for this lesson is shown in Listing 3.1.

LISTING 3.1   HTML Code Containing Markup for Lesson 3

```
<body>
<div id="content">
    <h1>
        Heading here
    </h1>
    <p class="intro">
        Lorem ipsum dolor sit amet.
    </p>
    <p>
        Lorem ipsum dolor <a href="#">sit</a> amet.
    </p>
</div>
<div id="nav">
    <ul>
        <li><a href="#" class="intro">item 1</a></li>
        <li><a href="#">item 2</a></li>
        <li><a href="#">item 3</a></li>
    </ul>
</div>
<div id="footer">
    Lorem ipsum dolor <a href="#">sit</a> amet.
</div>
</body>
```

What Is a `<div>`? The `<div>` element is a generic container that can be used to add structure to an HTML document. Although it is a block level element, it does not add any other presentation to the content.

For this lesson, the `<div>` element has been used to contain logical divisions of content, such as navigation and footer information.

These divisions of content can then be styled to suit your needs using descendant selectors, which are covered later in this lesson.

Type Selectors

Type selectors will select any HTML element on a page that matches the selector.

In the HTML sample shown in Listing 3.1, there are seven HTML elements that could be used as type selectors, including `<body>`, `<div>`, `<h1>`, `<p>`, `<ul>`, `<li>`, and `<a>`.

For example, to select all `<li>` elements on the page, the `<li>` selector is used as shown in Listing 3.2.

LISTING 3.2 CSS Code Containing Styling for the `<li>` Element

```
li
{
    color: blue;
}
```

Class Selectors

Class selectors can be used to select any HTML element that has been given a class attribute.

In the HTML sample shown in Listing 3.1, there are two HTML elements with class attributes—`<p class="intro">` and `<a href="#" class="intro">`.

For example, to select all instances of the `intro` class, the `.intro` selector is used as shown in Listing 3.3.

LISTING 3.3   CSS Code Containing Styling for the `.intro` Class

```
.intro
{
    font-weight: bold;
}
```

You also can select specific instances of a class by combining type and class selectors. For example, you might want to select the `<p class="intro">` and the `<a href="#" class="intro">` separately. This is achieved using `p.intro` and `a.intro` as shown in Listing 3.4.

LISTING 3.4   CSS Code Containing Two Different Stylings of the `.intro` Class

```
p.intro
{
    color: red;
}

a.intro
{
    color: green;
}
```

ID Selectors

ID selectors are similar to class selectors. They can be used to select any HTML element that has an ID attribute. However, each ID can be used only once within a document, whereas classes can be used as often as needed.

In this lesson, IDs are used to identify unique parts of the document structure, such as the content, navigation, and footer.

In the HTML sample shown in Listing 3.1, there are three IDs: `<div id="content">`, `<div id="nav">`, and `<div id="footer">`. To select `<div id="nav">`, the #nav selector is used as shown in Listing 3.5.

LISTING 3.5   CSS Code Containing the #nav ID Selector

```
#nav
{
    color: blue;
}
```

Should You Use ID or Class?   Classes can be used as many times as needed within a document. IDs can be applied only once within a document. If you need to use the same selector more than once, classes are a better choice.

However, IDs have more weight than classes. If a class selector and ID selector apply the same property to one element, the ID selector's value would be chosen. For example, h2#intro { color: red; } will override h2.intro { color: blue; }.

Descendant Selectors

Descendant selectors are used to select elements that are descendants of another element.

For example, in the HTML sample shown in Listing 3.1, three `<a>` elements are descendants of the `<li>` elements. To target these three `<a>` elements only, and not all other `<a>` elements, a descendant selector can be used as shown in Listing 3.6. This selector targets any `<a>` element that is nested inside an `<li>` element.

LISTING 3.6   CSS Code Containing Descendant Selector

```
li a
{
    color: green;
}
```

Descendant selectors do not have to use direct descendant elements. For example, the <a> element is a descendant of <div id="nav"> as well as the <li> element. This means that #nav a can be used as a selector as well (see Listing 3.7).

LISTING 3.7   CSS Code Containing Descendant Selector

```
#nav a
{
    color: red;
}
```

Descendant selectors also can include multiple levels of descendants to be more specific as shown in Listing 3.8.

LISTING 3.8   CSS Code Containing Descendant Selector

```
#nav ul li a
{
    color: green;
}
```

Universal Selectors

Universal selectors are used to select any element. For example, to set the margins and padding on every element to 0, * can be used as shown in Listing 3.9.

Listing 3.9   CSS Code Containing the Universal Selector

```
*
{
    margin: 0;
    padding: 0;
}
```

Universal selectors also can be used to select all elements within another element as shown in Listing 3.10. This will select any element inside the <p> element.

LISTING 3.10 CSS Code Containing the Universal Selector Within the <p> Element

```
p *
{
    color: red;
}
```

Advanced Selectors

Child selectors are used to select an element that is a direct child of another element (parent). Child selectors will not select all descendants, only direct children. For example, you might want to target an <em> that is a direct child of a <div>, but not other <em> elements that are descendants of the <div>. The selector is shown in Listing 3.11.

Child selectors are not supported by Windows Internet Explorer 5, 5.5, and 6, but are supported by most other standards-compliant browsers.

LISTING 3.11 CSS Code Containing the Child Selector

```
div > em
{
    color: blue;
}
```

Adjacent sibling selectors will select the sibling immediately following an element. For example, you might want to target an <h3> element, but only <h3> elements that immediately follow an <h2> element. This is a commonly used example because it has a real-world application. There is often too much space between <h2> and <h3> elements when they appear immediately after each other. The selector is shown in Listing 3.12.

Adjacent sibling selectors are not supported by Windows Internet Explorer 5, 5.5, and 6, but are supported by most other standards-compliant browsers.

LISTING 3.12   CSS Code Containing the Adjacent Sibling Selector

```
h2 + h3
{
    margin: -1em;
}
```

Attribute selectors are used to select elements based on their attributes or attribute value. For example, you might want to select any image on an HTML page that is called "small.gif" as shown in Listing 3.13.

Attribute selectors are not supported by Windows Internet Explorer 5, 5.5, and 6, or Macintosh Internet Explorer 5. They are also not supported by earlier versions of Opera.

LISTING 3.13   CSS Code Containing the Attribute Selector

```
img[src="small.gif"]
{
    border: 1px solid #000;
}
```

Pseudo-elements enable you to style information that is not available in the document tree. For instance, using standard selectors, there is no way to style the first letter or first line of an element's content. However, the content can be styled using pseudo-elements as shown in Listing 3.14.

Pseudo-elements :before and :after are not supported by Windows Internet Explorer 5, 5.5, and 6, or Macintosh Internet Explorer 5. They are also not supported by earlier versions of Opera.

LISTING 3.14   CSS Code Containing the Psuedo-Element Selector

```
p:first-line
{
    font-weight: bold;
}

p:first-letter
{
    font-size: 200%; font-weight: bold;}
```

Pseudo-classes enable you to format items that are not in the document tree. They include :first-child, :link, :visited, :hover, :active, :focus, and :lang(n). Pseudo-classes are covered in Lesson 10, "Styling Links."

Summary

In this lesson, you learned how to use a range of selectors, including type, class, ID, descendant, and universal. You also learned about the difference between ID and class selectors. In the next lesson, you will learn how to apply inline styles, header styles, and styles within external style sheets.

LESSON 4

Applying Styles

In this lesson, you will learn the three different locations where you can place CSS code, including inline, header, and external style sheets. You will also learn how to target a style sheet to a specific device such as a cell phone, television, or PDA by using media types. You will also learn methods that can be used to hide advanced styles from older browsers using media types.

Setting Up the HTML Code

The HTML code for this lesson that contains a single paragraph of text is shown in Listing 4.1.

LISTING 4.1 HTML Code Containing the Markup for Lesson 4

```
<!DOCTYPE HTML PUBLIC "-//W3C//DTD HTML 4.01//EN"
        "http://www.w3.org/TR/html4/strict.dtd">
<html lang="en">
<head>
    <meta http-equiv="content-type" content="text/html;
    charset=utf-8">
    <title>Lesson 4</title>
</head>
<body>
<p>
    Lorem ipsum dolor sit amet, consectetuer adipiscing
    elit...
</p>
</body>
</html>
```

In this lesson, the <p> element will be styled with font-family, width, background-color, margin, and padding.

These styles can be applied to <p> elements using three methods: *inline* styles, *header* styles, and *external* style sheets. Although each method will be explained, external style sheets are the preferred option because they do not add CSS to the HTML markup.

Applying Inline Styles

Inline styles can be applied directly to elements in the HTML code using the `style` attribute. However, inline styles should be avoided wherever possible because the styles are added to the HTML markup. This defeats the main purpose of CSS, which is to apply the same styles to as many pages as possible across your website using external style sheets. Styles that are applied inline can cause additional maintenance across a website because multiple pages might need changing rather than one CSS file.

An example of an inline style is shown in Listing 4.2.

LISTING 4.2   HTML Code Containing an Inline Style for the <p> Element

```
<!DOCTYPE HTML PUBLIC "-//W3C//DTD HTML 4.01//EN"
        "http://www.w3.org/TR/html4/strict.dtd">
<html lang="en">
<head>
    <meta http-equiv="content-type" content="text/html;
    charset=utf-8">
    <title>Lesson 4</title>
</head>
<body>
<p style="font-family: arial, helvetica, sans-serif; margin:
1em;padding: 1em; background-color: gray; width: 10em;">
    Lorem ipsum dolor sit amet, consectetuer adipiscing
    elit...
</p>
</body>
</html>
```

Using Header Styles

Header styles also can be used to style the <p> element. The CSS rules can be placed in the head of the document using the `style` element. Like inline styles, header styles should be avoided where possible because the styles are added to the HTML markup rather than in external CSS files.

There are cases where header styles might be the preferred option in specific instances, such as a CSS rule that is specific to one page within a large website. Rather than add this rule to an overall CSS file, a header style may be used.

An example of a header style is shown in Listing 4.3. The type= "text/css" attribute must be specified within the style element in order for browsers to recognize the file type.

LISTING 4.3   HTML Code Containing Header Styles

```
<!DOCTYPE HTML PUBLIC "-//W3C//DTD HTML 4.01//EN"
        "http://www.w3.org/TR/html4/strict.dtd">
<html lang="en">
<head>
    <meta http-equiv="content-type" content="text/html;
    charset=utf-8">
    <title>Lesson 4 - listing 2</title>
<style type="text/css" media="screen">
    p
    {
        font-family: arial, helvetica, sans-serif;
        margin: 1em;
        padding: 1em;
        background-color: gray;
        width: 10em;
    }
</style>
</head>
<body>
<p>
    Lorem ipsum dolor sit amet, consectetuer adipiscing
    elit...
</p>
</body>
</html>
```

Using External Style Sheets

The third method of applying styles to a document involves linking to external style sheets. External style sheets are the most appropriate method for styling documents. If styles need to be changed, the modifications can take place in one CSS file rather than all HTML pages.

To change the header style to an external style, move the rule set to a new CSS file as shown in Listing 4.4.

Next, link to this style sheet from your HTML file using the link element as shown in Listing 4.5.

LISTING 4.4   CSS Code Containing an External Style Sheet with Styles for the <p> Element

```
p
{
    font-family: arial, helvetica, sans-serif;
    margin: 1em;
    padding: 1em;
    background-color: gray;
    width: 10em;
}
```

LISTING 4.5   HTML Code Containing the link Element

```
<!DOCTYPE HTML PUBLIC "-//W3C//DTD HTML 4.01//EN"
         "http://www.w3.org/TR/html4/strict.dtd">
<html lang="en">
<head>
    <meta http-equiv="content-type" content="text/html;
    charset=utf-8">
    <title>Lesson 4</title>
    <link rel="stylesheet" href="style.css" type="text/css"
    media="screen">
</head>
<body>
<p>
    Lorem ipsum dolor sit amet, consectetuer adipiscing
    elit...
</p>
</body>
</html>
```

@import Styles

Header and external style sheets also can import other style sheets using the @import rule as shown in Listing 4.6. The @import rule must be placed before all other rules in the header or external style sheet.

LISTING 4.6   CSS Code Containing an Imported Style Sheet

```
@import "advanced.css";

p
{
    font-family: arial, helvetica, sans-serif;
    margin: 1em;
    padding: 1em;
    background-color: gray;
    width: 10em;
}
```

Imported styles can be used to link to multiple CSS files as well as to hide styles from older browsers.

Hiding Styles from Older Browsers

Some older browsers, such as Netscape Navigator 4 and Internet Explorer 4, have poor support for CSS. It is possible to hide styles from these browsers using specific media types and @import rules.

All styles will be hidden from Netscape Navigator 4 by changing the link element's media type from screen to screen, projection as shown in Listing 4.7. Netscape Navigator 4 does not support multiple media types.

LISTING 4.7   HTML Code Containing a link Element with a screen, projection Media Type

```
<!DOCTYPE HTML PUBLIC "-//W3C//DTD HTML 4.01//EN"
        "http://www.w3.org/TR/html4/strict.dtd">
<html lang="en">
<head>
        <meta http-equiv="content-type" content="text/html;
        charset=utf-8">
        <title>Lesson 4</title>
```

continues

```
<link rel="stylesheet" href="style.css" type="text/css"
media="screen, projection">
</head>
<body>
<p>
        Lorem ipsum dolor sit amet, consectetuer adipiscing
        elit...
</p>
</body>
</html>
```

The remaining styles will be hidden from Internet Explorer 4 and several
other older browsers by moving the <p> element rule set out of the original style sheet and into the imported style sheet as shown in Listings 4.8
and 4.9. Internet Explorer 4 is not able to read imported files.

**LISTING 4.8   CSS Code Inside the Original Style Sheet Called
style.css**

```
@import "advanced.css";
```

**LISTING 4.9   CSS Code Inside the Import Style Sheet Called
advanced.css**

```
p
{
    font-family: arial, helvetica, sans-serif;
    margin: 1em;
    padding: 1em;
    background-color: gray;
    width: 10em;
}
```

All modern browsers will read the multiple media type screen,
projection, as well as the imported style, so they will display the
fully styled <p> element.

Header styles also can be hidden from older browsers by enclosing the
contents of the style element inside a comment as shown in Listing 4.10.

LISTING 4.10   HTML Code Containing Header Styles Within a Comment

```
<style type="text/css" media="screen">
<!--
    p
    {
        font-family: arial, helvetica, sans-serif;
        margin: 1em;
        padding: 1em;
        background-color: gray;
        width: 10em;
    }
-->
</style>
```

Summary

In this lesson, you learned how to apply inline, header, and external styles to a document. You also learned what a media type is and how to hide advanced styles from older browsers using multiple media types and @import. In the next lesson, you will learn about the CSS box model including margin, background color, background image, padding, and border.

LESSON 5

Getting to Know the CSS Box Model

In this lesson, you will learn about the CSS box model—the rectangular boxes that are generated for all HTML elements. You will learn about aspects that make up the box model, including margin, background color, background image, padding, and border. You also will learn the difference between inline and block level elements.

Understanding Inline and Block Level Elements

Block level elements are normally displayed as blocks with line breaks before and after. Examples of block level elements include paragraphs, headings, divs, and block quotes.

Inline elements are not displayed as blocks. The content is displayed in lines and there are no line breaks before and after. Examples of inline elements include emphasized text, strong text, and links. Examples of both block and inline elements are shown in Figure 5.1.

This is a heading ⊢ Block level <h1> element

Lorem ipsum dolor sit amet, consectetuer adipiscing elit, ⊢ Block level <p> element
sed diam nonummy **nibh euismod** tincidunt ut laoreet ⊢ Inline <strong> element
dolore magna aliquam erat volutpat. Ut wisi enim ad minim
veniam, quis nostrud *exerci tation ullamcorper* suscipit ⊢ Inline <em> element
lobortis nisl ut aliquip ex ea commodo consequat. Nulla
facilisis at vero eros et accumsan et iusto odio dignissim ⊢ Inline <a> element
qui blandit praesent luptatum zzril delenit augue duis.

FIGURE 5.1 Examples of block level and inline elements.

All block level and inline elements are boxes that use the box model. Both types of elements can be styled with box model properties such as margin, background-color, background-image, padding, and border as shown in Figure 5.2.

Some box model properties, such as height and width, do not apply to inline elements. Also, margin and padding applied to an inline element will affect content on either side, but not content above or below.

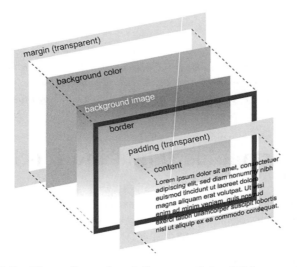

FIGURE 5.2   Three-dimensional diagram of the CSS box model.

Setting Box Width

The width of an element is applied to the content area. Other measurements, such as padding, border, and margins, are added to this width.

For example, if an element is specified with width: 200px;, the content area is 200px wide. If padding, border, or margin are applied to the same element, their measurements are added to the overall width.

However, Internet Explorer 5 for Windows (and Internet Explorer 6 for Windows in some circumstances) will use a different method to set widths for boxes. If padding and border are applied to an element, their measurements are subtracted from the overall width. This is shown in Figure 5.3.

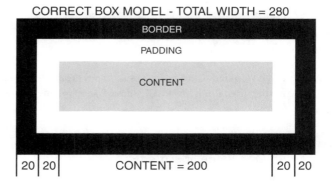

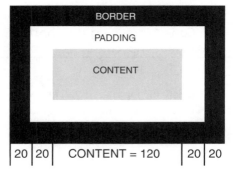

FIGURE 5.3   CSS box model showing Internet Explorer width problem.

Margins

Margins can be applied to the outside of any block level or inline element. They create space between the edge of an element and the edge of any adjacent elements.

Margins can be applied to individual sides of a box as shown in Listing 5.1.

LISTING 5.1   CSS Code Containing Various `margin` Properties

```
p { margin-top: 0; }
p { margin-right: 2em; }
h2 { margin-bottom: 3em; }
h3 { margin-left: 1em; }
```

Margins also can be applied using a single shorthand property. If one `margin` value is specified, it applies to all sides of an element as shown in Listing 5.2.

LISTING 5.2   CSS Code Containing the `margin` Shorthand Property with One Value Specified

```
p { margin: 1em; }
```

If two values are specified, the top and bottom margins are set to the first value and the right and left margins are set to the second as shown in Listing 5.3.

LISTING 5.3   CSS Code Containing the Shorthand `margin` Property with Two Values Specified

```
p { margin: 1em 0; }
```

If three values are specified, the top is set to the first value, the left and right are set to the second, and the bottom is set to the third as shown in Listing 5.4.

LISTING 5.4   CSS Code Containing the Shorthand `margin` Property with Three Values Specified

```
p { margin: 1em 0 2em; }
```

If four values are specified, they apply to the top, right, bottom, and left as shown in Listing 5.5.

LISTING 5.5   CSS Code Containing the Shorthand `margin` Property with Four Values Specified

```
p { margin: 1em 2em 2em 1em; }
```

Background Color and Background Image

The background-color property sets the background color of an element.

The background-image property applies a background image to an element, which will appear on top of any background-color. Background images are covered in more detail in Lesson 6, "Adding Background Images."

Padding

Padding can be applied to the outside edges of the content area of any block level or inline element. Padding creates the space between the edge of the element and its content.

Like margins, padding can be applied to individual sides of a box as shown in Listing 5.6.

LISTING 5.6 CSS Code Containing Various padding Properties

```
p { padding: 1em; }
h1 { padding-top: 0; }
h2 { padding-right: 2em; }
h2 { padding-bottom: 3em; }
h3 { padding-left: 1em; }
```

Padding also can be applied using a single shorthand property. If one padding value is specified, it applies to all sides of an element as shown in Listing 5.7.

LISTING 5.7 CSS Code Containing the Shorthand padding Property with One Value Specified

```
p { padding: 1em; }
```

If two values are specified, the top and bottom margins are set to the first value and the right and left margins are set to the second as shown in Listing 5.8.

LISTING 5.8 CSS Code Containing the Shorthand `padding` Property with Two Values Specified

```
p { padding: 1em 0; }
```

If three values are specified, the top is set to the first value, the left and right are set to the second, and the bottom is set to the third as shown in Listing 5.9.

LISTING 5.9 CSS Code Containing the Shorthand `margin` Property with Three Values Specified

```
p { padding: 1em 0 2em; }
```

If four values are specified, they apply to the top, right, bottom, and left as shown in Listing 5.10.

LISTING 5.10 CSS Code Containing the Shorthand `padding` Property with Four Values Specified

```
p { padding: 1em 2em 2em 1em; }
```

Border

The `border` properties specify the width, color, and style of the border of an element. Shorthand `border` properties include `border-top`, `border-bottom`, `border-right`, `border-left`, and `border` as shown in Listing 5.11.

LISTING 5.11 CSS Code Containing Various Shorthand `border` Properties

```
p { border-top: 1px solid red; }
p { border-right 1px solid red; }
p { border-bottom: 1px solid red; }
p { border-left: 1px solid red; }
p { border: 1px solid red; }
```

Content Area

The content area of a box can be given width, height, and color. Width and height can be specified in points (equal to 1/72 of an inch), picas (equal to 12 points), pixels, ems, exes, millimeters, centimeters, inches, or percents as shown in Listing 5.12.

LISTING 5.12   CSS Code Containing Various `width` and `height` Values

```
p { width: 100pt; }
p { height: 20pc; }
p { width: 300px; }
p { height: 40em; }
p { width: 50ex; }
p { height: 600mm; }
p { width: 70cm; }
p { height: 8in; }
p { width: 50%; }
```

The `color` property can be used to style the text color. Color can be specified in a number of ways, including keywords, hexadecimal RGB, and functional notation RGB.

Keywords for `color` include aqua, black, blue, fuchsia, gray, green, lime, maroon, navy, olive, purple, red, silver, teal, white, and yellow. Although other keywords might work in some browsers, they are not part of the specification and should not be used.

Hexadecimal colors can be specified using only three or six hexadecimal characters as shown in Listing 5.13. When a color has three pairs of hexadecimal digits (such as `#ff0000`), it can be shortened by removing one digit from each pair (`#f00`). RGB colors can be specified using three comma-separated integer or percentage values. For example, the color red can be specified using either `rgb(255, 0, 0)` or `rgb(100%, 0%, 0%)` as shown in Listing 5.13.

LISTING 5.13   CSS Code Containing Various `color` Values

```
p { color: red }
p { color: #f00 }
p { color: #ff0000 }
p { color: rgb(255,0,0) }
p { color: rgb(100%, 0%, 0%) }
```

Summary

In this lesson, you learned about the CSS box model including margin, background color, background image, padding, and border. You also learned the difference between inline and block level elements and how some versions of Internet Explorer misinterpret the box model. In the next lesson, you will learn how to apply a background image to the <body> element. You also will learn how to apply the background-repeat and background-position properties.

LESSON 6

Adding Background Images

In this lesson, you will learn how to apply a background image to the
<body> element. You will also learn how to apply the `background-repeat`
and `background-position` *properties. The aim is to create a gradient*
image that repeats down the right edge of the page.

Setting Up the HTML Code

The HTML code for this lesson will be comprised of three paragraphs of
text as shown in Listing 6.1.

LISTING 6.1 HTML Code Containing the Markup for
Lesson 6

```
<p>
    Lorem I
psum dolor sit amet...
</p>
<p>
    Ut wisi enim ad minim veniam...
</p>
<p>
    Duis autem vel eum iriure dolor...
</p>
```

Creating Selectors to Style the Header

To style the `<body>` element and its content, you will only need a single type selector as shown in Listing 6.2.

LISTING 6.2   CSS Code Showing the Selector to Style the Body

```
body {...}
```

Adding `background-image`

The `background-image` property is used to add a background image to the `<body>` element.

Values for the `background-image` property are either a `url` (to specify the image) or `none` (when no image is used).

For this lesson, you will use `url(chapter6.jpg)`. The image path can be written with or without quotation marks. The `background-image` code is shown in Listing 6.3. The results can be seen in Figure 6.1.

LISTING 6.3   CSS Code Styling the `<body>` Element with a Background Image

```
body
{
    background-image: url(chapter6.jpg);
}
```

 Background Images and Internet Explorer 5 for Macintosh   Internet Explorer 5 for Macintosh will not render `background-images` if quotations are used around image paths. Because quotation marks are not needed, it is simpler and safer to leave them out.

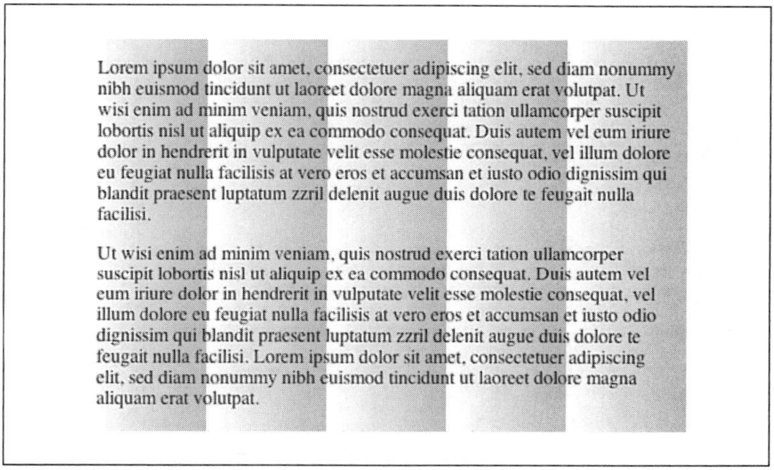

FIGURE 6.1   Screenshot of styled <body>.

Setting `background-repeat`

The background image in this lesson is now repeating across the screen. This can be controlled using `background-repeat`.

Values for the `background-repeat` property (see Figure 6.2) include `repeat` (where the image is repeated both horizontally and vertically), `repeat-x` (where the image is repeated horizontally only), `repeat-y` (where the image is repeated vertically only), and `no-repeat` (where the image is not repeated).

In this lesson, you will use `repeat-y`, as shown in Listing 6.4, to force the image to repeat vertically down the page.

LISTING 6.4   CSS Code Setting `background-repeat`

```
body
{
    background-image: url(chapter6.jpg);
    background-repeat: repeat-y;
}
```

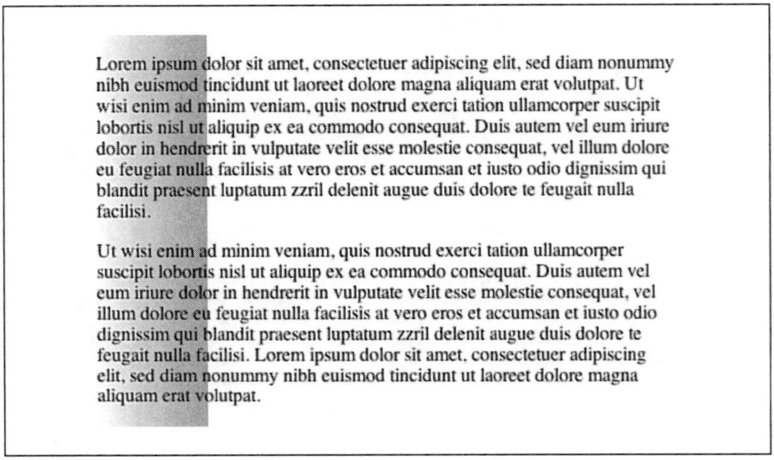

Lorem ipsum dolor sit amet, consectetuer adipiscing elit, sed diam nonummy nibh euismod tincidunt ut laoreet dolore magna aliquam erat volutpat. Ut wisi enim ad minim veniam, quis nostrud exerci tation ullamcorper suscipit lobortis nisl ut aliquip ex ea commodo consequat. Duis autem vel eum iriure dolor in hendrerit in vulputate velit esse molestie consequat, vel illum dolore eu feugiat nulla facilisis at vero eros et accumsan et iusto odio dignissim qui blandit praesent luptatum zzril delenit augue duis dolore te feugait nulla facilisi.

Ut wisi enim ad minim veniam, quis nostrud exerci tation ullamcorper suscipit lobortis nisl ut aliquip ex ea commodo consequat. Duis autem vel eum iriure dolor in hendrerit in vulputate velit esse molestie consequat, vel illum dolore eu feugiat nulla facilisis at vero eros et accumsan et iusto odio dignissim qui blandit praesent luptatum zzril delenit augue duis dolore te feugait nulla facilisi. Lorem ipsum dolor sit amet, consectetuer adipiscing elit, sed diam nonummy nibh euismod tincidunt ut laoreet dolore magna aliquam erat volutpat.

FIGURE 6.2   Screenshot of `<body>` styled with `background-repeat`.

Adding `background-position`

Now that the background image is repeating correctly, it must be positioned down the right edge of the `<body>` element. This is achieved using `background-position`.

Values for the `background-position` property include `percentage` (such as `0 100%`), `length` (such as `2px 20px`), and `keywords` (such as `left top`). In each case, the horizontal position is specified first, and then the vertical position. The values `0% 0%` will position the upper-left corner of the image in the upper-left corner of the box's padding edge. Values of `0 100%` will position the bottom-left corner of the image in the bottom-left corner of the box's padding edge. Values of `2px 20px` will position the top-left corner of the image `2px` in from the left edge of the box and `20px` down from the top of the box.

If only one percentage or length value is given, it sets the horizontal position only and the vertical position will be `50%`. If two values are given, the horizontal position comes first. Combinations of length and percentage values are allowed (such as `50% 2cm`). Negative positions are also allowed (such as `-20px 10px`).

For this lesson, you will use percentage values of 100% 0, which will place the image in the right and top of the element. The code is shown in Listing 6.5.

The image will now repeat down the right edge of the <body> element (see Figure 6.3).

Background Position Issues   Some browsers do not recognize the background-position keyword value right. However, all modern browsers support the percentage value of 100%, so this value can be used instead.

LISTING 6.5   CSS Code Styling the <body> Element with background-position

```
body
{
    background-image: url(chapter6.jpg);
    background-repeat: repeat-y;
    background-position: 100% 0;
}
```

Lorem ipsum dolor sit amet, consectetuer adipiscing elit, sed diam nonummy nibh euismod tincidunt ut laoreet dolore magna aliquam erat volutpat. Ut wisi enim ad minim veniam, quis nostrud exerci tation ullamcorper suscipit lobortis nisl ut aliquip ex ea commodo consequat. Duis autem vel eum iriure dolor in hendrerit in vulputate velit esse molestie consequat, vel illum dolore eu feugiat nulla facilisis at vero eros et accumsan et iusto odio dignissim qui blandit praesent luptatum zzril delenit augue duis dolore te feugait nulla facilisi.

Ut wisi enim ad minim veniam, quis nostrud exerci tation ullamcorper suscipit lobortis nisl ut aliquip ex ea commodo consequat. Duis autem vel eum iriure dolor in hendrerit in vulputate velit esse molestie consequat, vel illum dolore eu feugiat nulla facilisis at vero eros et accumsan et iusto odio dignissim qui blandit praesent luptatum zzril delenit augue duis dolore te feugait nulla facilisi. Lorem ipsum dolor sit amet, consectetuer adipiscing elit, sed diam nonummy nibh euismod tincidunt ut laoreet dolore magna aliquam erat volutpat.

FIGURE 6.3   Screenshot of <body> element styled with background-position.

Using the background Shortcut

As discussed in Lesson 2, "Using CSS Rules," shorthand properties allow the values of several properties to be specified within a single property. The background property can be used to combine background-color, background-image, background-repeat, background-attachment, and background-position.

When sorting shorthand properties, browsers will first set all the individual properties to their initial values, and then override these with values specified by the author.

A default background rule would be set to background: transparent none repeat scroll 0 0;. If the declarations used in this lesson are combined into the shorthand rule, they will override the default values for background-image, background-repeat, and background-position. The result will be background: transparent url(chapter6.jpg) repeat-y scroll 100% 0;.

However, the rule can be shortened to include only the values that are needed, so the final declaration will be background: url(chapter6.jpg) repeat-y 100% 0; (see Listing 6.6).

LISTING 6.6   CSS Code Styling the <body> Element with a Shorthand background Property

```
body
{
    background: url(chapter6.jpg) repeat-y 100% 0;
}
```

Adding padding

The final step will be to add padding to the <body> element to push the text away from the background-image. This can be achieved using the shorthand padding declaration padding: 1em 80px 1em 1em; as shown in Listing 6.7. This will place 1em of padding on the top, bottom, and left of the <body> and 80px on the right edge. The results can be seen in Figure 6.4.

LISTING 6.7   CSS Code Adding `padding` to the `<body>` Element

```
body
{
    background: url(chapter6.jpg) repeat-y 100% 0;
    margin: 0;
    padding: 1em 80px 1em 1em;
}
```

Lorem ipsum dolor sit amet, consectetuer adipiscing elit, sed diam nonummy nibh euismod tincidunt ut laoreet dolore magna aliquam erat volutpat. Ut wisi enim ad minim veniam, quis nostrud exerci tation ullamcorper suscipit lobortis nisl ut aliquip ex ea commodo consequat. Duis autem vel eum iriure dolor in hendrerit in vulputate velit esse molestie consequat, vel illum dolore eu feugiat nulla facilisis at vero eros et accumsan et iusto odio dignissim qui blandit praesent luptatum zzril delenit augue duis dolore te feugait nulla facilisi.

Ut wisi enim ad minim veniam, quis nostrud exerci tation ullamcorper suscipit lobortis nisl ut aliquip ex ea commodo consequat. Duis autem vel eum iriure dolor in hendrerit in vulputate velit esse molestie consequat, vel illum dolore eu feugiat nulla facilisis at vero eros et accumsan et iusto odio dignissim qui blandit praesent luptatum zzril delenit augue duis dolore te feugait nulla facilisi. Lorem ipsum dolor sit amet, consectetuer adipiscing elit, sed diam nonummy nibh euismod tincidunt ut laoreet dolore magna aliquam erat volutpat.

FIGURE 6.4   Screenshot of `<body>` element with `padding` applied.

Summary

In this lesson, you learned how to apply a background image to the `<body>` element. You also learned how to apply the `background-repeat`, `background-position`, and shorthand `background` properties. In the next lesson, you will learn how to style text using the `font`, `size`, `color`, and `alignment` properties.

LESSON 7
Formatting Text

In this lesson, you will learn how to style text using font, size, alignment, and color properties instead of the <font> element.

Setting Up the HTML Code

The HTML code for this lesson contains three paragraphs of text as shown in Listing 7.1. The contents of these paragraphs are wrapped inside <font> elements. The first paragraph has been set to a larger font size. It also has been colored and styled in bold and italic. The results are shown in Figure 7.1.

LISTING 7.1   HTML Code Containing Markup for Lesson 7

```
<p align="center">
    <font size="4" color="#990000" face="times, times new
    roman">
    <b><i>Lorem ipsum dolor sit amet, consectetuer adipiscing
    elit...</i></b></font>
</p>
<p>
    <font size="2" face="arial, helvetica">
    Ut wisi enim ad minim
veniam, quis nostrud exerci...</font>
</p>
<p>
    <font size="2" face="arial, helvetica">
    Duis autem vel eum iriure dolor in hendrerit vulputate...
    </font>
</p>
<p>
    <font size="2" face="arial, helvetica"><p> nostrud
    exerci...
    </font>
</p>
```

Lorem ipsum dolor sit amet, consectetuer adipiscing elit, sed diam nonummy nibh euismod tincidunt ut laoreet dolore magna aliquam erat volutpat. Ut wisi enim ad minim veniam quis nostrud exerci tation ullamcorper suscipit lobortis nisl ut aliquip ex ea commodo.

Ut wisi enim ad minim veniam, quis nostrud exerci tation ullamcorper suscipit lobortis nisl ut aliquip ex ea commodo consequat. Duis autem vel eum iriure dolor in hendrerit culputate velit esse molestie consequat, vel illum dolore eu feugiat nulla facilisis ero eros et accumsan et iusto odio dignissim qui blandit praesent luptatum zzril.

Duis autem vel eum iriure dolor in hendrerit in vulputate velit esse molestie consequat, vel illum dolore eu feugiat nulla facilisis at vero eros et accumsan et iusto odio dignissim qui blandit praesent luptatum zzril delenit augue duis dolore te feugait nulla facilisi. Lorem ipsum dolor sit amet, consectetuer adipiscing elit, sed diam nonummy nibh euismod tincidunt ut laoreet dolore magna aliquam erat volutpat.

FIGURE 7.1 Screenshot of `<font>`-styled paragraphs.

Removing Font Elements

Instead of using `<font>` elements throughout a document, you should use CSS to style the content. This reduces the overall file size and makes future maintenance easier. All font-styling information can be stored in one external file, rather than scattered throughout every document in a website.

The `<font>` elements will be removed from the HTML markup as shown in Listing 7.2. The first paragraph will be styled with an `introduction` class because it will need additional styling (see Figure 7.2).

LISTING 7.2   HTML Code Containing the Markup Without
`<font>` Elements

```
<p class="introduction">
    Lorem ipsum dolor sit amet, consectetuer adipiscing
    elit...
</p>
<p>
    Ut wisi enim ad minim veniam, quis nostrud exerci...
</p>
<p>
    Duis autem vel eum iriure dolor in hendrerit vulputate...
</p>
    Ut wisi enim ad minim veniam, quis nostrud exerci...
</p>
```

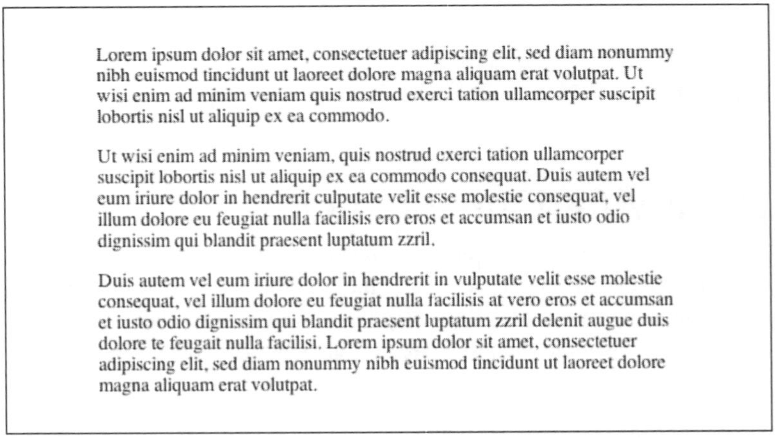

Lorem ipsum dolor sit amet, consectetuer adipiscing elit, sed diam nonummy nibh euismod tincidunt ut laoreet dolore magna aliquam erat volutpat. Ut wisi enim ad minim veniam quis nostrud exerci tation ullamcorper suscipit lobortis nisl ut aliquip ex ea commodo.

Ut wisi enim ad minim veniam, quis nostrud exerci tation ullamcorper suscipit lobortis nisl ut aliquip ex ea commodo consequat. Duis autem vel eum iriure dolor in hendrerit culputate velit esse molestie consequat, vel illum dolore eu feugiat nulla facilisis ero eros et accumsan et iusto odio dignissim qui blandit praesent luptatum zzril.

Duis autem vel eum iriure dolor in hendrerit in vulputate velit esse molestie consequat, vel illum dolore eu feugiat nulla facilisis at vero eros et accumsan et iusto odio dignissim qui blandit praesent luptatum zzril delenit augue duis dolore te feugait nulla facilisi. Lorem ipsum dolor sit amet, consectetuer adipiscing elit, sed diam nonummy nibh euismod tincidunt ut laoreet dolore magna aliquam erat volutpat.

FIGURE 7.2   Screenshot of paragraphs with `<font>` elements removed.

Creating the Selectors

To style the paragraphs, two selectors will be used as shown in Listing 7.3.

LISTING 7.3   CSS Code Showing the Selectors to Style
the Paragraphs

```
p {...}
p.introduction {...}
```

Styling the <p> Element

The font family is set using the font-family property. A range or fonts should always be included, separated by commas. A generic font family must be included at the end of the list. If a user does not have the initial font family, his or her browser will look for the second font family. If no font family matches are found, the browser will fall back to the generic font family.

 Generic Font Families   Generic font families are a fallback mechanism to provide some basic font styling if none of the specified font families are available. The five generic font families are serif, sans-serif, cursive, fantasy, and monospace.

The font-size property will be set to 80%, which will make it 80% of the user's default browser style. Using percentages will allow the user to control the overall size of fonts (see Figure 7.3).

 Ems and Percents   In theory, there is no difference between using ems or percents for font sizing. However, Internet Explorer 5 for Windows will misread em measurements below 100% and change the unit from ems to pixels. For example, a value of .8em will be displayed at 8px.

To avoid this problem, font-size should be set using percentage units for any value below 100%.

Finally, a line-height of 140% will be included to provide space between each line and make the text more readable. The default line-height for most browsers is 120%. Setting a value of 140% will add 20% additional space between each line. The rule set is shown in Listing 7.4.

Listing 7.4   CSS Code Containing Styles for the `<p>` Element

```
p
{
    font-family: arial, helvetica, sans-serif;
    font-size: 80%;
    line-height: 140%;
}
```

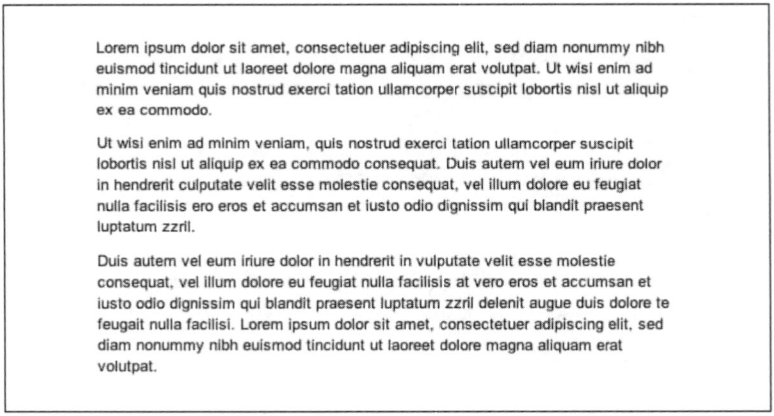

Lorem ipsum dolor sit amet, consectetuer adipiscing elit, sed diam nonummy nibh euismod tincidunt ut laoreet dolore magna aliquam erat volutpat. Ut wisi enim ad minim veniam quis nostrud exerci tation ullamcorper suscipit lobortis nisl ut aliquip ex ea commodo.

Ut wisi enim ad minim veniam, quis nostrud exerci tation ullamcorper suscipit lobortis nisl ut aliquip ex ea commodo consequat. Duis autem vel eum iriure dolor in hendrerit culputate velit esse molestie consequat, vel illum dolore eu feugiat nulla facilisis ero eros et accumsan et iusto odio dignissim qui blandit praesent luptatum zzril.

Duis autem vel eum iriure dolor in hendrerit in vulputate velit esse molestie consequat, vel illum dolore eu feugiat nulla facilisis at vero eros et accumsan et iusto odio dignissim qui blandit praesent luptatum zzril delenit augue duis dolore te feugait nulla facilisi. Lorem ipsum dolor sit amet, consectetuer adipiscing elit, sed diam nonummy nibh euismod tincidunt ut laoreet dolore magna aliquam erat volutpat.

FIGURE 7.3   Screenshot of styled paragraphs.

Styling the First Paragraph

The first paragraph in this example will use different fonts than the other paragraphs. In this case, it will be styled with `times`, `"times new roman"`, `serif`. Fonts such as Times New Roman, which have spaces in their names, should always be wrapped in quotation marks.

The next step is to style the text italic and bold. This is achieved using `font-style: italic;` and `font-weight: bold;`.

To align the text in the center of the screen, use `text-align: center`.

The font size can be increased using `font-size: 110%;` and the font color can be set using `color: #900;` as shown in Listing 7.5 (see Figure 7.4).

LISTING 7.5   CSS Code Containing Styles for the First Paragraph

```
p
{
    font-family: arial, helvetica, sans-serif;
    font-size: 80%;
    line-height: 1.4;
}

p.introduction
{
    font-family: times, "times new roman", serif;
    font-style: italic;
    font-weight: bold;
    text-align: center;
    font-size: 110%;
    color: #900;
}
```

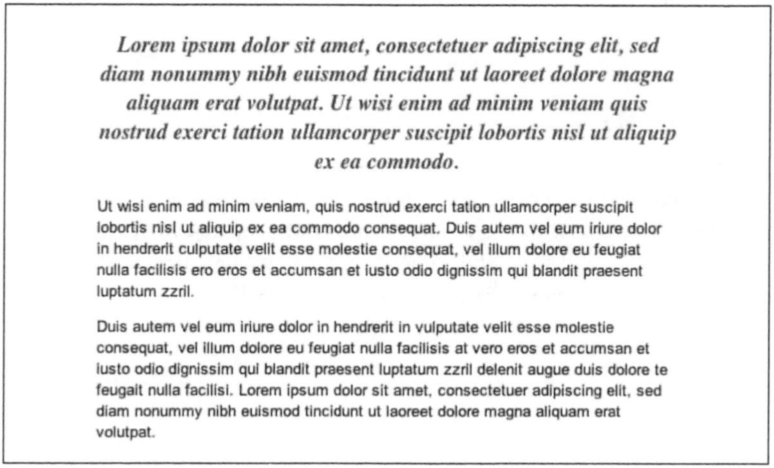

Lorem ipsum dolor sit amet, consectetuer adipiscing elit, sed diam nonummy nibh euismod tincidunt ut laoreet dolore magna aliquam erat volutpat. Ut wisi enim ad minim veniam quis nostrud exerci tation ullamcorper suscipit lobortis nisl ut aliquip ex ea commodo.

Ut wisi enim ad minim veniam, quis nostrud exerci tation ullamcorper suscipit lobortis nisl ut aliquip ex ea commodo consequat. Duis autem vel eum iriure dolor in hendrerit culpatate velit esse molestie consequat, vel illum dolore eu feugiat nulla facilisis ero eros et accumsan et iusto odio dignissim qui blandit praesent luptatum zzril.

Duis autem vel eum iriure dolor in hendrerit in vulputate velit esse molestie consequat, vel illum dolore eu feugiat nulla facilisis at vero eros et accumsan et iusto odio dignissim qui blandit praesent luptatum zzril delenit augue duis dolore te feugait nulla facilisi. Lorem ipsum dolor sit amet, consectetuer adipiscing elit, sed diam nonummy nibh euismod tincidunt ut laoreet dolore magna aliquam erat volutpat.

FIGURE 7.4   Screenshot of styled first paragraph.

Converting to Shorthand

As discussed in Lesson 2, "Using CSS Rules," shorthand properties are easier to write and maintain than longhand properties. They also make CSS files more concise.

The <p> element can be styled so that font-size, line-height, and font-family are declared as a single font property.

The introduction class can be styled so that font-style, font-weight, font-size, line-height, and font-family are declared as a single font property as shown in Listing 7.6.

LISTING 7.6   CSS Code Containing the Shorthand Styles

```
p
{
    font: 80%/1.4 arial, helvetica, sans-serif;
}

p.introduction
{
    font: bold italic 110%/1.4 times, "times new roman",
serif;
    text-align: center;
    color: #900;
}
```

Summary

In this lesson, you learned how to style text using font-family, font-size, line-height, font-style, font-weight, text-align, and color. You also learned how to use the shorthand font property. In the next lesson, you will learn how to style a heading using border, background-images, and text-transform properties.

LESSON 8
Styling a Flexible Heading

In this lesson, you will learn how to create a border above and below a heading, add a continuous gradient background image, and style the text with text-transform *and letter spacing.*

Styling the Heading

To style this heading, you will need a selector that targets the <h1> element. To make sure you don't target every <h1> on the page, you should also include a unique identifier, such as header, within the selector (see Listing 8.1).

LISTING 8.1 CSS Code Showing the Selector to Style the Heading

```
h1#header {...}
```

The HTML code used for this heading is shown in Listing 8.2.

LISTING 8.2 HTML Code Containing the Markup for a Heading

```
<h1 id="header">
    Page Heading
</h1>
```

Heading Levels and Document Structure   Web documents should use semantically correct markup to add meaning to the content. For example, headings should be placed inside heading elements, paragraphs of text should be placed inside paragraph elements, and lists should be placed inside list elements.

When the semantically correct HTML markup is in place, CSS can be used to visually style the content.

Heading levels are an important part of this markup. Ideally, web pages should start with a single <h1> element for the most significant information on the page, such as the page title or the site name.

Headings should never be faked using <font> or <strong> elements because they do not provide meaning for devices such as screen readers or text-based browsers.

Adding Color, Font Size, and Weight

To add a color to the heading, use the color property. The color can be changed to suit your needs.

For this heading, you will set the font-size to 120% and the font-weight to normal, as shown in Listing 8.3.

LISTING 8.3   CSS Code Setting font-size and font-weight

```
h1#header
{
    color: #036;
font-size: 120%;
    font-weight: normal;
}
```

Overriding Standard Heading Settings Any HTML document may have three or more style sheets associated with it, including a *browser* style sheet, a *user* style sheet, and one or more *author* style sheets.

Browsers apply default style sheets to all web documents. Although these browser style sheets vary from browser to browser, they have common characteristics, such as black text and blue links.

Most modern browsers allow users to set their own style sheets within their browser. These user style sheets will override any browser default style sheets—for that user only.

As soon as you apply a basic style sheet or an inline style to a page, you have added an author style sheet. Author style sheets will generally override both browser and user style sheets.

Most browser style sheets will display an <h1> element in bold text at 200% of the default font size. If you style the <h1> element to 120%, this measurement will be used instead of 200% because your style sheet will override the browser style sheet.

 Using Shorthand Hexadecimal Colors Hexadecimal colors can be specified using the # symbol immediately followed by three or six hexadecimal characters.

Three-digit hexadecimal values are converted to six-digit form by replicating digits. So, #f00 is the same as #ff0000 and #f2a is the same as #ff22aa.

Setting Text Options

The next step is to center the heading, make it uppercase, and add some letter spacing. This can be achieved using the text-transform, text-align, and letter-spacing properties as shown in Listing 8.4 and illustrated in Figure 8.1. These options can be changed to suit your needs.

LISTING 8.4   CSS Code Transforming Text

```
h1#header
{
    color: #036;
    font-size: 120%;
    font-weight: normal;
    text-transform: uppercase;
    text-align: center;
    letter-spacing: .5em;
}
```

```
                        PAGE   HEADING
```

FIGURE 8.1   Screenshot of uppercase, centered heading.

Applying Padding and Borders

Later in this lesson, you will be adding borders to the top and bottom of the heading. To avoid placing the text hard against the borders, you will need to add some top and bottom padding. You can use the shorthand padding property, setting top and bottom padding to .4em, and left and right padding to 0.

To apply borders to the top and bottom of the heading, use the border-top and border-bottom properties as shown in Listing 8.5.

The results can be seen in Figure 8.2. The borders can be removed or changed to suit your needs.

LISTING 8.5   CSS Code Adding Borders

```
h1#header
{
    color: #036;
    font-size: 120%;
    font-weight: normal;
    text-transform: uppercase;
    text-align: center;
    letter-spacing: .5em;
    padding: .4em 0;
    border-top: 1px solid #069;
    border-bottom: 1px solid #069;
}
```

PAGE HEADING

FIGURE 8.2   Screenshot of bordered heading.

 CSS Borders   CSS Border properties define the borders around an element.

`border-color` sets the color of the border (for example, red, transparent, none, #036, #003366).

`border-width` sets the thickness of the border (for example, thin, medium, thick, 1px, .5em, 1ex).

`border-style` sets the appearance of the border (for example, none, hidden, dotted, dashed, solid, double, groove, ridge, inset, outset).

Border properties and values can be specified in many ways. The simplest option is to use the shorthand `border` property like this:

```
border: (width) (style) (color);
```

Some border styles, such as `dotted`, are not supported by Internet Explorer 5 or 5.5.

Adding a Background Image

To add a background image to the heading, use the background property. You can then specify the url and the repeat value as shown in Listing 8.6. In this case, the image is set to repeat-x, so it will repeat across the x axis only.

The results can be seen in Figure 8.3. The background image can be removed or changed to suit your needs.

Listing 8.6   CSS Code Adding a Background Image

```
h1#header
{
    color: #036;
    font-size: 120%;
    font-weight: normal;
    text-transform: uppercase;
    text-align: center;
    letter-spacing: .5em;
    padding: .4em 0;
    border-top: 1px solid #069;
    border-bottom: 1px solid #069;
    background: url(chapter8.jpg) repeat-x;
}
```

PAGE HEADING

Figure 8.3   Screenshot of finished heading.

Summary

In this lesson, you have learned how to style a flexible heading using font-size, font-weight, borders, padding, and background images. In the next lesson, you will learn how to style a round-cornered heading.

LESSON 9
Styling a Round-Cornered Heading

In this lesson, you will learn how to wrap a round-cornered box around a heading. The box is made from two background images that adjust to suit any size heading.

Styling the Heading

To style this heading, you will need a selector that targets the <h2> element. To make sure you don't target every <h2> on the page, you should also include a class within the selector. A class is used in this case instead of an ID because you might want to include more than one of these fixed-width headings on a single page (see Listing 9.1).

LISTING 9.1 CSS Code Showing the Selectors to Style the Heading

```
h2.decorative {...}
h2.decorative em {...}
```

The HTML code used for this heading is shown in Listing 9.2. Notice that the heading is wrapped inside an <em> (emphasis) element. This additional element will be important later in the lesson.

LISTING 9.2   HTML Code Containing the Markup for a Heading

```
<h2 class="decorative">
    <em>Section Heading</em>
</h2>
```

 Creating the Scaleable Background Image   The heading in this lesson will eventually be wrapped inside a round-cornered box.

This box must be able to grow downward if the heading text is long, or if the user has chosen to use larger font sizes within her browser.

For this reason, the round-cornered box is made up of two background images. The first image is the top section of the box, and the second image is the bottom section of the box.

The first image must be very long, in order to grow downward as needed.

If the first background image is applied to the <h2> element, the second background image must be applied to another element.

One simple option is to wrap the heading text in an <em> element and apply the second image to this. As long as the second image is positioned at the bottom of the <em> element, the content can grow as needed.

Styling the <h2> Element

To add a color to the <h2> element, use the color property. The color can be changed to suit your needs.

The font weight, size, and family are set using the font property, and the heading is centered using the text-align property as shown in Listing 9.3 and illustrated in Figure 9.1.

LISTING 9.3   CSS Code Setting Text Alignment

```
h2.decorative
{
    color: #036;
    font: bold 100% arial, helvetica, sans-serif;
    text-align: center;
}
```

Section Heading

FIGURE 9.1   Screenshot of styled heading.

Adding a Background Image

To add a background image to the `<h2>` element, use the `background` property. The image should be set to `no-repeat` so it doesn't reappear in the middle of a long heading. The image is shown in Figure 9.2.

FIGURE 9.2   Screenshot of the first image—which is applied to the `<h2>` element.

You will also need to set a `width` for this element because the background image is 220 pixels wide. If the width is left undefined, the heading will poke out the side of the round-cornered box.

You should also apply 5 pixels of `padding` on the top of the element as shown in Listing 9.4 and illustrated in Figure 9.3. This top padding will move the text down slightly so it doesn't sit hard against the background image.

LISTING 9.4 CSS Code Setting Background Image, Width, and Padding

```
h2.decorative
{
    color: #036;
    font: bold 100% arial, helvetica, sans-serif;
    text-align: center;
    background: url(chapter9.gif) no-repeat;
    width: 220px;
    padding: 5px 0 0 0;
}
```

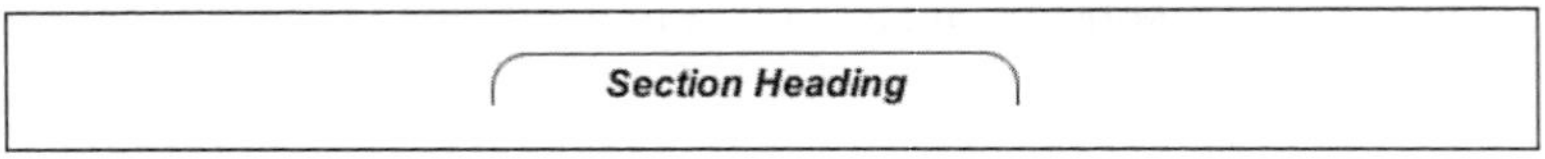

```
                    Section Heading
```

FIGURE 9.3 Screenshot of heading with background image.

Styling the <em> Element

The <em> element will be used to house the second background image—the bottom of the round-cornered box. This means it must be given the same width as the <h2> element in order for the two images to line up properly.

However, because the <em> is an inline element, it will ignore any width that is specified. The solution is to set it to display: block; before applying a width.

Next, padding-bottom is used to move the text up slightly so it doesn't sit hard against the background image.

You can also override the <em> element's default italic style using font-style: normal;.

Finally, you need to apply the background image using the background property. The image should be set to no-repeat so it does not reappear under the heading. The background position should be set to 0 100% so the lower-left corner of the image will align with the lower-left corner of the element's edge.

The image is shown in Figure 9.4 and the CSS code is shown in Listing 9.5. The completed heading is shown in Figure 9.5.

FIGURE 9.4 Screenshot of the second image—which is applied to the <em> element.

LISTING 9.5 CSS Code Styling the <em> Element

```
h2.decorative
{
    color: #036;
    font: bold 100% arial, helvetica, sans-serif;
    text-align: center;
    background: url(chapter9.gif) no-repeat;
    width: 220px;
    padding: 5px 0 0 0;
}

h2.decorative em
{
    display: block;
    width: 220px;
    padding: 0 0 5px 0;
    font-style: normal;
    background: url(chapter9a.gif) no-repeat 0 100%;
}
```

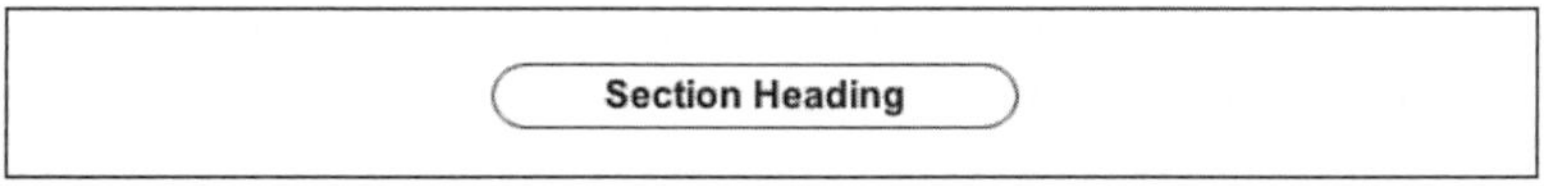

> (Section Heading)

FIGURE 9.5 Screenshot of the final heading.

Summary

In this lesson, you have learned how to apply color, font, and text alignment to a heading. You have also learned how to set background images for two elements in order to achieve a round-corner box. In the next lesson you will learn about styling links.

LESSON 10
Styling Links

In this lesson, you will learn how to style links. You also will learn how to add background images to links, turn off link underlines, use borders for underlines, and increase the active link area.

Links and Pseudo-Classes

You have already learned how to style <a> or link elements in Lesson 3, "Selectors in Action." Now you will learn how to style the five different link states.

Links can be in the following states:

- **Normal**—The standard unvisited link state

- **Visited**—The link points to a URI that has already been visited

- **Hover**—The cursor is over the active area of the link

- **Active**—The moment the link is selected or clicked

- **Focus**—The link is in focus and ready to accept input, such as a click or mouse down

Some link states cannot occur at the same time. For example, a link can either be visited or unvisited—it cannot be both. However, visited and unvisited links can also be in the hover, active, and focus states.

Each of these states can be styled individually using link pseudo-classes (classes that do not exist in the document structure). The five link pseudo-classes are

- `a:link`—Styles unvisited link elements

- `a:visited`—Styles visited link elements

- `a:focus`—Styles the state during focus

- `a:hover`—Styles the state when the cursor moves over a link

- `a:active`—Styles the state when a link is activated

The five pseudo-classes are shown in Listing 10.1.

LISTING 10.1   CSS Code Containing the Five Link Pseudo-Classes

```
a:link    {...}
a:visited {...}
a:focus   {...}
a:hover   {...}
a:active  {...}
```

 Focus and Active States   The `a:focus` pseudo-class highlights the tab position for people who use a keyboard to navigate.

Unfortunately, Internet Explorer for Windows does not support the `a:focus` pseudo-class. Instead, it uses the `a:active` pseudo-class for tab highlighting.

As an additional problem, Internet Explorer for Windows incorrectly applies the `a:active` pseudo-class. The `a:active` state remains visible until another action takes place.

Setting Pseudo-Class Order

The five pseudo-classes have the same weight, so the order in which they are placed within a CSS file is important. Pseudo-class declarations that appear later in a CSS file will override those that appear earlier. The correct order is shown in Listing 10.2.

LISTING 10.2 CSS Code Containing Correct Order of <a> Pseudo-Classes

```
a {...}
a:link   {...}
a:visited   {...}
a:focus   {...}
a:hover   {...}
a:active   {...}
```

Using Classes with Pseudo-Classes

Class selectors can be combined with pseudo-classes to create links for different purposes. For example, you might want to style links depending on whether they are internal or external.

A class could be added to all external links, and then these links could be styled using a combined class and pseudo-class selector as shown in Listing 10.3. The results can be seen in Figure 10.1.

LISTING 10.3 CSS Code Demonstrating Combined Class and Pseudo-Class Selectors

```
a:link
{
    color: blue;
}

a:visited
{
    color: purple;
}

a.external:link
{
    color: red;
    font-weight: bold;
}

a.external:visited
{
    color: black;
    font-weight: bold;
}
```

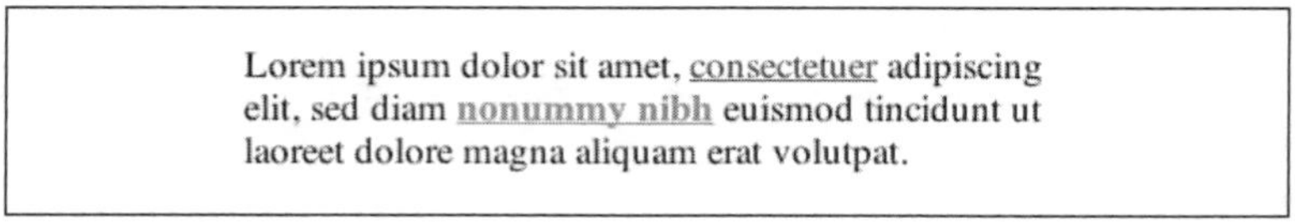

Lorem ipsum dolor sit amet, consectetuer adipiscing
elit, sed diam nonummy nibh euismod tincidunt ut
laoreet dolore magna aliquam erat volutpat.

FIGURE 10.1   Screenshot showing difference between a:link and
a.external:link.

Styling Links with Background Images

Following on from the preceding example, it is possible to display a small icon beside every external link.

The first step is to create basic rules for the required link states. In this case, you can use a:link, a:visited, and a:hover.

Three new states are then added, specifically for links styled with an "external" class. These are a.external:link, a.external:visited, and a.external:hover.

In each case, a background image is added to the link. The image is set to no-repeat so that it doesn't tile across the background of the entire link. The position is set to 100%, which will place the right edge of the image against the right edge of the link.

A single background image is used for all three states. The vertical background-position needs to change for each state. This means that a single image is loaded and cached, so there is no lag when the rollover image is required.

The a:link state has been set to 0. The a:visited state has been set to -100px. The a:hover state has been set to -200px. The background image is shown in Figure 10.2.

Finally, padding has been used to push the link content away from the background image as shown in Listing 10.4 (see Figure 10.3).

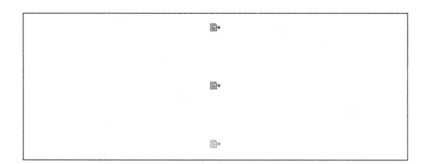

FIGURE 10.2   Screenshot of background image used to style the `.external` link.

LISTING 10.4   CSS Code Containing the Markup to Style the `.external` Link

```
a:link
{
    color: blue;
}

a:visited
{
    color: purple;
}

a:hover
{
    color: red;
}

a.external:link
{
    background: url(chapter10.gif) no-repeat 100% 0;
    padding-right: 20px;
}

a.external:visited
{
    background: url(chapter10.gif) no-repeat 100% -100px;
    padding-right: 20px;
}

a.external:hover
```

continues

```
{
    background: url(chapter10.gif) no-repeat 100% -200px;
    padding-right: 20px;
}
```

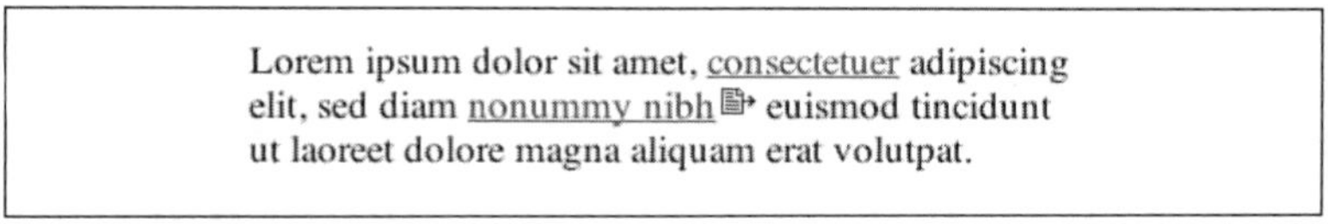

> Lorem ipsum dolor sit amet, consectetuer adipiscing
> elit, sed diam nonummy nibh 🖹 euismod tincidunt
> ut laoreet dolore magna aliquam erat volutpat.

Figure 10.3   Screenshot showing styled .external link with a background image.

Removing Underlines and Applying Borders

Some users, particularly those with poor eyesight, might find standard link underlines hard to read. This is particularly true for links that contain italic text.

One solution is to turn off text underlines and use borders.

The first step is to set the text-decoration to none. This will turn off link underlines.

Next, the required states need to be colored. In this case, a:link is set to blue, a:visited is set to purple, and a:hover is set to red.

Finally, borders are added to each state using border-bottom as shown in Listing 10.5. padding-bottom can be added to control the distance between the underline and the content, if required (see Figure 10.4).

Listing 10.5   CSS Code to Style Links with Borders

```
a
{
    text-decoration: none;
}

a:link
{
```

continues

LISTING 10.5   Continued

```
    color: blue;
    border-bottom: 1px solid blue;
}

a:visited
{
    color: purple;
    border-bottom: 1px solid purple;
}

a:hover
{
    color: red;
    border-bottom: 1px solid red;
}
```

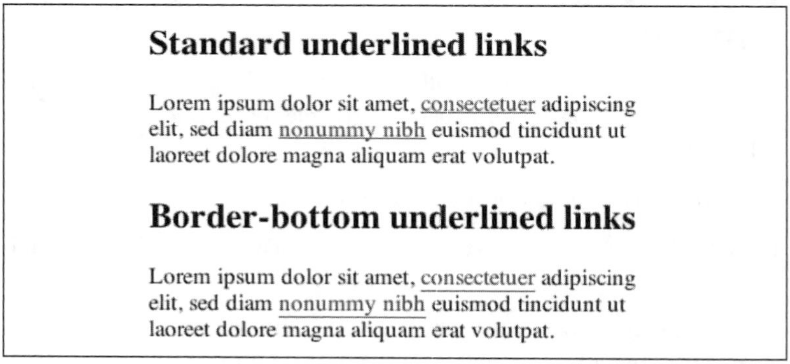

Standard underlined links

Lorem ipsum dolor sit amet, consectetuer adipiscing
elit, sed diam nonummy nibh euismod tincidunt ut
laoreet dolore magna aliquam erat volutpat.

Border-bottom underlined links

Lorem ipsum dolor sit amet, consectetuer adipiscing
elit, sed diam nonummy nibh euismod tincidunt ut
laoreet dolore magna aliquam erat volutpat.

FIGURE 10.4   Screenshot showing difference between links with
underlines and links with border-bottom.

Increasing the Active Area of Links

For some users, particularly those with motor-skill difficulties, clicking on
links can be difficult. Using CSS, the active area of links can be increased.

The first step is to add .5em of padding above and below the <a> element
to increase the active area of a link. This is achieved using padding:
.5em 0;.

Next, the <a> element should be set to position: relative, which will stop the padding from affecting surrounding text, as shown in Listing 10.6 (see Figure 10.5).

To see the increased link area in action, you can apply a background color to the <a> element. This background color can be removed before it is applied in a real situation.

A more detailed explanation of this technique is available on David Benton's website at http://www.dbenton.com/go/chronicles/2004/08/22/fitts-law-and-text-links/.

LISTING 10.6   CSS Code Containing Styles to Increase the Active Area of Links

```
a
{
    padding: .4em 0;
    position:relative;
    z-index: 1;
    background: yellow;
}
```

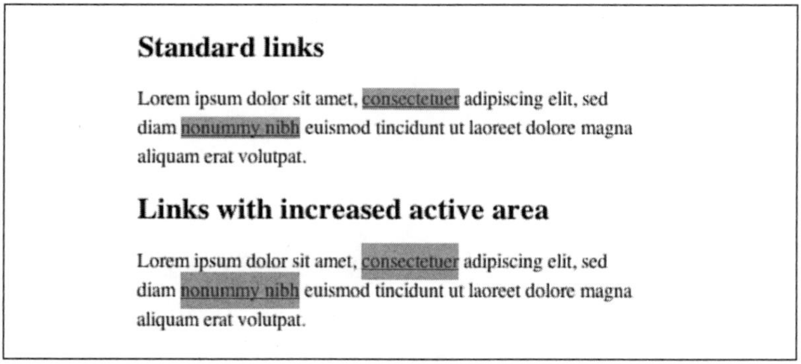

Standard links

Lorem ipsum dolor sit amet, consectetuer adipiscing elit, sed diam nonummy nibh euismod tincidunt ut laoreet dolore magna aliquam erat volutpat.

Links with increased active area

Lorem ipsum dolor sit amet, consectetuer adipiscing elit, sed diam nonummy nibh euismod tincidunt ut laoreet dolore magna aliquam erat volutpat.

FIGURE 10.5   Screenshot showing difference between standard link area and links with increased active area.

Summary

In this lesson, you learned how to style links and pseudo-classes. You learned how to apply background images and borders to the <a> element. You also learned how to increase the active area of links to make them more accessible. In the next lesson, you will learn how to position and style an image and its caption.

LESSON 11

Positioning an Image and Its Caption

In this lesson, you will learn how to position and style an image and its caption.

Wrapping the Image and Caption

The first step is to wrap a container around the image and caption so they can be floated together. There are many elements that can be used such as paragraphs, lists, or even definition lists. However, for this lesson, you will use a `<div>` as shown in Listing 11.1.

LISTING 11.1   HTML Code Containing the Markup for a Container, an Image, and Its Caption

```
<div class="imagecaption">
    <img src="chapter11a.gif" alt="">
    A flower from my garden.
</div>
<p>
    Lorem ipsum dolor sit amet...
</p>
```

To make sure you don't target every `<div>` on the page, you should include a class within the selector as shown in Listing 11.2.

A class is used here instead of an ID because you might want to include more than one floated image and caption on a page.

LISTING 11.2   CSS Code Showing the Selectors for Styling the Container

```
div.imagecaption {...}
div.imagecaption img {...}
```

Floating the Container

To move the container across to the right edge of the browser window, use `float: right`.

When the container is floated, it must be given a width. In this case, you will use `width: 182px`.

Why the strange width? The image inside of this container is 180px wide. Later in this lesson, the image will be given a 1px-wide border. The right border width (`1px`), left border width (`1px`), and image width (`180px`) add up to `182px`.

Next, you might want to create some space around the container so that text and other elements don't butt up against it (see Figure 11.1). You can achieve this by applying margins to the right, bottom, and left of the container as shown in Listing 11.3.

LISTING 11.3   CSS Code Floating the Container

```
div.imagecaption
{
    float: right;
    width: 182px;
    margin: 0 1em 1em 1em;
    display: inline;
}
```

Lorem ipsum dolor sit amet, consectetuer adipiscing elit, sed diam nonummy nibh euismod tincidunt ut laoreet dolore magna aliquam erat volutpat. Ut wisi enim ad minim veniam, quis nostrud exerci tation ullamcorper suscipit lobortis nisl ut aliquip ex ea commodo consequat. Duis autem vel eum iriure dolor in hendrerit in vulputate velit esse molestie consequat, vel illum dolore eu feugiat nulla facilisis at vero eros et accumsan et iusto odio dignissim qui blandit praesent luptatum zzril delenit augue duis dolore te feugait nulla facilisi.

A flower from my garden.

FIGURE 11.1   Screenshot of floated container.

Floats, Margins, and Internet Explorer 5 If you view samples from this lesson in Internet Explorer 5 and 5.5 for Windows, you will notice that the right margin is actually much wider than in other browsers. In fact, it is 2em wide—double the width it is supposed to be. This is Internet Explorer's Double Margin Float Bug.

This bug occurs when you apply a right margin to a right floated element and it sits directly against the right edge of the parent container.

The opposite is also true. The bug will occur when you apply a left margin to a left floated element and it sits against the left edge of the parent container.

Luckily, there is a solution. Simply add `display: inline` to the rule set. All other browsers will ignore this declaration, but Internet Explorer 5 and 5.5 for Windows will then apply the correct margin width.

Applying Padding, Background Color, and a Background Image

Now that the container is positioned, you can style its appearance using padding, background-image, and background color.

The first step is to apply padding to the container to create space around the image and caption. You can use the shorthand padding rule to specify values for top, right, bottom, and left. All sides should be given a value of 10px except the bottom, which should be given a value of 70px. This will provide some space for the background image.

The background image can be applied using background-image: url(chapter11.gif) as shown in Figure 11.2.

You must set a repeat value to avoid the image repeating across the entire background area of the container. In this case, you will need the image to repeat across the x-axis. This is achieved using background-repeat: repeat-x.

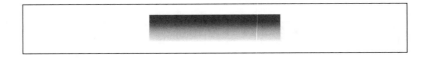

FIGURE 11.2   Screenshot of background image.

The background image needs to be aligned with the bottom of the container. One way to achieve this is to set the `vertical` value to `100%`, which will place the bottom of the image against the bottom of the padding area. The declaration would be `background-position: 0 100%`.

The background color can be specified using `background-color: #036`.

All of these `background` declarations can be condensed into one shorthand declaration as shown in Listing 11.4. The results are illustrated in Figure 11.3.

LISTING 11.4   CSS Code Setting Padding, Background Color, and Background Image

```
div.imagecaption
{
    float: right;
    width: 182px;
    margin: 0 1em 1em 1em;
    display: inline;
    padding: 10px 10px 70px 10px;
    background: #036 url(chapter11.gif) repeat-x 0 100%;
}
```

FIGURE 11.3   Screenshot of container with padding and background.

Background Position Keywords   When you position a background image, you can use measurements (for example, 1em, 20%, and 5px) or you can use keywords (left, right, center, top, and bottom).

Unfortunately, some versions of Internet Explorer and Opera for Windows ignore keywords.

Luckily, these can be replaced with percentage values that have exactly the same effect.

If you want to position a background image at the right of a container, you can use a horizontal value of 100%. This will align the right edge of the image with the right edge of the container.

If you want to position a background image at the bottom of a container, you can use a vertical value of 100%. This will align the bottom edge of the image with the bottom edge of the container.

Styling the Caption

The next step is to apply some basic styles to the caption text, starting with color.

There are many ways that the color white can be specified, including white, #fff, #ffffff, rgb(255,255,255), and rgb(100%,100%,100%). In this case, the three-digit hexadecimal option will be used—color: #fff.

Text can be aligned to the left, right, center, or justify. This caption will be centered using text-align: center as shown in Listing 11.5. The results can be seen in Figure 11.4.

LISTING 11.5   CSS Code Styling the Caption

```
div.imagecaption
{
    float: right;
    width: 182px;
```

continues

LISTING **11.5**   Continued

```
    margin: 0 1em 1em 1em;
    display: inline;
    padding: 10px 10px 70px 10px;
    background: #036 url(chapter11.gif) repeat-x 0 100%;
    color: #fff;
    text-align: center;
}
```

Lorem ipsum dolor sit amet, consectetuer adipiscing elit, sed diam nonummy nibh euismod tincidunt ut laoreet dolore magna aliquam erat volutpat. Ut wisi enim ad minim veniam, quis nostrud exerci tation ullamcorper suscipit lobortis nisl ut aliquip ex ea commodo consequat. Duis autem vel eum iriure dolor in hendrerit in vulputate velit esse molestie consequat, vel illum dolore eu feugiat nulla facilisis at

A flower from my garden.

FIGURE 11.4   Screenshot of styled caption.

Styling the Image

Finally, the image can be styled with a border.

There are many ways to specify a border around an image. The simplest method is the shorthand `border` property shown in Listing 11.6 and illustrated in Figure 11.5.

LISTING **11.6**   CSS Code Styling the Image

```
div.imagecaption
{
    float: right;
    width: 182px;
    margin: 0 1em 1em 1em;
    display: inline;
    padding: 10px 10px 70px 10px;
    background: #036 url(chapter11.gif) repeat-x 0 100%;
    color: #fff;
    text-align: center;
}
```

continues

```
div.imagecaption img
{
    border: 1px solid #fff;
}
```

Lorem ipsum dolor sit amet, consectetuer adipiscing elit, sed diam nonummy nibh euismod tincidunt ut laoreet dolore magna aliquam erat volutpat. Ut wisi enim ad minim veniam, quis nostrud exerci tation ullamcorper suscipit lobortis nisl ut aliquip ex ea commodo consequat. Duis autem vel eum iriure dolor in hendrerit in vulputate velit esse molestie consequat, vel illum dolore eu feugiat nulla facilisis at

A flower from my garden.

FIGURE 11.5   Screenshot of the final result.

Creating a Side-By-Side Variation

Using the same selectors and HTML code, it is possible to change the layout to display the image and caption side by side.

First, the width of the container will need to be increased to accommodate the new caption and image locations. The declaration can be changed to width: 302px. This width can be changed to suit your needs.

Next, padding can be set to 10px for all sides because you do not need any space for a background image.

The background-image, background-repeat, and background-position properties can also be removed, leaving a simple declaration—background: #036.

The image must be floated to the right so that the caption can sit beside it. Width does not need to be defined in this case because the image has its own intrinsic width.

Finally, the image will need to be given some margin so that the caption doesn't butt up against it. You can use margin-right: 1em as shown in Listing 11.7 and illustrated in Figure 11.6.

LISTING 11.7   CSS Code for the Side-By-Side Variation

```
div.imagecaption
{
    float: right;
    width: 302px;
    margin: 0 1em 1em 1em;
    display: inline;
    padding: 10px;
    background: #036;
    color: #fff;
}

div.imagecaption img
{
    float: right;
    margin-left: 1em;
    border: 1px solid #fff;
}
```

FIGURE 11.6   Screenshot of the side-by-side variation.

Creating a Photo Frame Variation

Another variation is to create a simple photo frame using the container and some borders.

The first step is to change the padding to 15px for top, right, and left edges, and 20px for the bottom. Like the original example, this additional space will be used for the background image.

The borders will be used to create a three-dimensional illusion. The top
and left edges will have light-colored thin borders, whereas the right and
bottom edges will have darker and thicker borders. This can be achieved
using three border declarations as shown in Listing 11.8.

LISTING 11.8   CSS Code for the Photo Frame Variation

```
div.imagecaption
{
    float: right;
    width: 182px;
    margin: 0 1em 1em 1em;
    padding: 15px 15px 20px 15px;
    display: inline;
    text-align: center;
    border-color: #CCC #999 #999 #CCC;
    border-width: 1px 2px 2px 1px;
    border-style: solid;
    background: url(chapter11c.gif) repeat-x 0 100%;
}

div.imagecaption img
{
    border-color: #000 #ccc #ccc #000;
    border-width: 1px 1px 1px 1px;
    border-style: solid;
}
}
```

A new background image can be used with the same settings as the original version.

Finally, borders need to be added to the image. These borders will be set
in the opposite colors to the container, with darker borders on the top and
left edges of the image, and lighter borders on the right and bottom edges.

The final results can be seen in Figure 11.7.

Lorem ipsum dolor sit amet, consectetuer adipiscing elit, sed diam nonummy nibh euismod tincidunt ut laoreet dolore magna aliquam erat volutpat. Ut wisi enim ad minim veniam, quis nostrud exerci tation ullamcorper suscipit lobortis nisl ut aliquip ex ea commodo consequat. Duis autem vel eum iriure dolor in hendrerit in vulputate velit esse molestie consequat, vel illum dolore eu feugiat nulla facilisis at vero eros et accumsan et iusto odio dignissim qui blandit praesent luptatum zzril delenit augue duis dolore te feugait nulla facilisi.

A flower from my garden.

FIGURE 11.7   Screenshot of the photo frame variation.

Summary

In this lesson, you have learned how to wrap a container around an image and its caption. You then learned how to float the container and style it with width, margin, padding, background image, color, and text-align. You also learned how to apply borders to the image. In the next lesson, you will learn how to create a photo gallery.

LESSON 12

Creating a Photo Gallery

In this lesson, you will learn how to create a photo gallery using a series of floated <div> elements. You will also learn how to use two backgrounds images to create a flexible container.

Creating a Thumbnail Gallery

First of all, you will need a series of thumbnail images and captions. Each thumbnail image and caption will be placed inside a <div> element. The caption will then be placed inside a <p> element as shown in Listing 12.1.

To make sure you don't target every <div> on the page, you should apply the same classname to each one.

LISTING 12.1 HTML Code Containing the Markup for a Thumbnail Gallery

```
<div class="thumbnail">
    <img src="chapter12c.jpg" alt="">
    <p>A flower from my garden</p>
</div>
<div class="thumbnail">
    <img src="chapter12c.jpg" alt="">
    <p>White and pinkflower in Spring</p>
</div>
<div class="thumbnail">
    <img src="chapter12c.jpg" alt="">
    <p>Flower in morning light</p>
</div>
<div class="thumbnail">
    <img src="chapter12c.jpg" alt="">
    <p>A close-up of flower petals</p>
</div>
```

continues

LISTING 12.1   Continued

```
<div class="thumbnail">
    <img src="chapter12c.jpg" alt="">
    <p>A timeless flower </p>
</div>
```

You will be using three selectors in this lesson. The first selector will target any `<div>` that contains a `"thumbnail"` class.

The second selector will target any image inside a `<div>` that contains a `"thumbnail"` class.

The third selector will target any `<p>` element inside a `<div>` that contains a `"thumbnail"` class. The selectors are shown in Listing 12.2.

LISTING 12.2   CSS Code Showing the Selectors for Styling the Container

```
div.thumbnail {...}
div.thumbnail img {...}
div.thumbnail p {...}
```

Positioning the `<div>` Elements

Because the images and captions will sit beside each other in rows, you will need to float the `<div>`. This can be achieved using `float: left`.

When the `<div>` is floated, it must be given a width. In this case, you will use `width: 130px`. This width can be changed to suit your needs.

Next, you might want to create some space around the `<div>` elements so that they don't butt up against each other. You can achieve this by applying margins to the right and bottom of each `<div>`.

Finally, a background image (shown in Figure 12.1) will be added to the `<div>`. As you can see in Figure 12.1, the image is very long so that it is able to grow to accommodate long captions.

This background image must be set to `no-repeat` because you don't want it to reappear under the caption. The CSS code is shown in Listing 12.3 and illustrated in Figure 12.2.

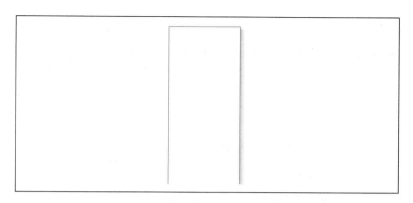

FIGURE 12.1   Screenshot of background image used by `<div>` element.

LISTING 12.3   CSS Code Floating the Container

```
div.thumbnail
{
    width: 130px;
    float: left;
    margin: 0 10px 10px 0;
    background: url(chapter12a.gif) no-repeat;
}
```

FIGURE 12.2   Screenshot of positioned containers.

Liquid and Fixed-Width Layouts The floated `<div>` elements you have created will sit in a line beside each other, depending on the width of your browser window.

If you decrease the width of your browser, one or more `<div>` elements may drop to a new line below.

This happens because the `<div>` elements have no container apart from the browser window. This type of layout is referred to as a *liquid layout*.

However, you can stop the `<div>` elements from dropping to new lines. If you place them inside a fixed-width container, they will remain in position—no matter how narrow the browser window. This type of layout is referred to as a *fixed-width layout*.

Styling the Image

At present, the image sits hard against the edge of its container, the `<div>` element. To give it some space, you can set margins on the top and left using `margin: 10px 0 0 10px`.

You can also add a border to the image using `border: 1px solid #777` as shown in Listing 12.4. The results can be seen in Figure 12.3.

LISTING 12.4   CSS Code for Styling the Image

```
div.thumbnail
{
    width: 130px;
    float: left;
    margin: 0 10px 10px 0;
    background: url(chapter12a.gif) no-repeat;
}

div.thumbnail img
{
    margin: 10px 0 0 10px;
    border: 1px solid #777;
}
```

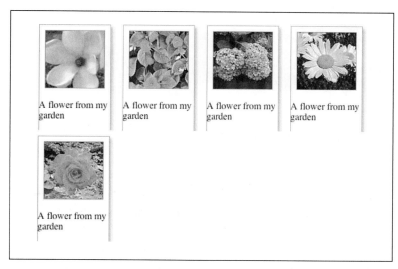

FIGURE 12.3 Screenshot of styled image.

Styling the Paragraph Element

Most browsers render standard `<p>` elements with margins of 1em above and below. You can override these margins using `margin: 0`.

Now the paragraph will sit under the image, but it is still sitting against the edge of its container. You will need to give it some space using padding. In this case, apply `20px` of padding to the right, `30px` below, and `10px` to the left.

Next, you need to add a background image to finish off the illusion of the drop-shadow box. This image (shown in Figure 12.4) will sit at the bottom of the `<p>` element.

Set the image to `no-repeat` so it doesn't reappear in a long caption. The vertical background position should be set to `100%`, which will make the bottom of the image sit against the bottom of the `<p>` element. The code is shown in Listing 12.5 and illustrated in Figure 12.5.

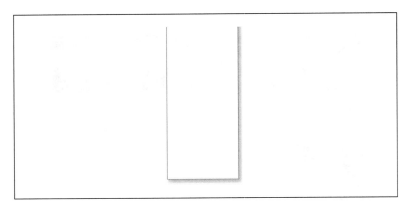

FIGURE 12.4   Screenshot of background image used by <p> element.

LISTING 12.5   CSS Code for Styling the <p> Element

```
div.thumbnail
{
    width: 130px;
    float: left;
    margin: 0 10px 10px 0;
    background: url(chapter12a.gif) no-repeat;
}

div.thumbnail img
{
    border: 1px solid #777;
    margin: 10px 0 0 10px;
}

div.thumbnail p
{
    margin: 0;
    padding: 0 20px 30px 10px;
    background: url(chapter12b.gif) no-repeat 0 100%;
}
```

FIGURE 12.5   Screenshot of final thumbnail gallery.

Forcing a New Line

There may be situations when you want to set a number of thumbnails on each line. To do this, you need to create a new class and then apply this class to specific <div> elements. The new class will have one declaration—clear: left. This will move the <div> down to a new line, below the bottom edge of any previous left-floating <div> elements. The CSS code is shown in Listing 12.6.

LISTING 12.6   CSS Code Forcing a New Line

```
div.thumbnail
{
    width: 130px;
    float: left;
    margin: 0 10px 10px 0;
    background: url(chapter12a.gif) no-repeat;
}

div.thumbnail img
{
```

continues

LISTING 12.6   Continued

```
    border: 1px solid #777;
    margin: 10px 0 0 10px;
}

div.thumbnail p
{
    margin: 0;
    padding: 0 20px 30px 10px;
    background: url(chapter12b.gif) no-repeat 0 100%;
}

.clear
{
    clear: left;
}
```

This new class will need to be added to any <div> that must start on a new line. The simplest way to add this new class is to include it in the existing class attribute. So, class="thumbnail" can be changed to class="thumbnail clear" as shown in Listing 12.7. The final results can be seen in Figure 12.6.

LISTING 12.7   HTML Code Showing New Class

```
<div class="thumbnail">
    <img src="chapter12c.jpg" alt="">
    <p>A flower from my garden</p>
</div>
<div class="thumbnail">
    <img src="chapter12c.jpg" alt="">
    <p>A flower from my garden</p>
</div>
<div class="thumbnail">
    <img src="chapter12c.jpg" alt="">
    <p>A flower from my garden</p>
</div>
<div class="thumbnail clear">

    <img src="chapter12c.jpg" alt="">
    <p>A flower from my garden</p>
</div>
<div class="thumbnail">
```

continues

```
<img src="chapter12c.jpg" alt="">
<p>A flower from my garden</p>
</div>
```

FIGURE 12.6   Screenshot of thumbnail gallery.

Creating a Side-By-Side Variation

Using the same selectors and HTML code, it is possible to change the layout so that the images and their captions are displayed side by side.

First, the width of the `<div>` will need to be increased to accommodate the caption beside the image. The declaration can be changed to `width: 250px`.

Next, some `padding-bottom` and a `border` can be added to the `<div>`.

The `background` declaration can be removed completely.

The image must be floated to the left so that the caption can sit beside it. Width does not need to be defined in this case because the image has its own intrinsic width.

Finally, the image will need to be given some margin so that the caption doesn't butt up against it. You can use `10px` for all sides except the bottom as shown in Listing 12.8. The results can be seen in Figure 12.7.

LISTING 12.8   CSS Code for the Side-By-Side Variation

```
div.thumbnail
{
    float: left;
    width: 250px;
    margin: 0 10px 10px 0;
    padding-bottom: 10px;
    border: 1px solid #777;
}

div.thumbnail img
{
    float: left;
    border: 1px solid #777;
    margin: 10px 10px 0 10px;
}

div.thumbnail p
{
    margin: 0;
    padding: 10px;
}
```

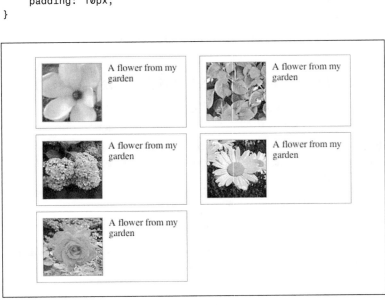

FIGURE 12.7   Screenshot of the side-by-side variation.

Summary

In this lesson, you have learned to float a series of `<div>` elements, and then style them. You also learned how to force a line break using `clear`.

In the next lesson, you will learn how to style a blockquote.

LESSON 13
Styling a Block Quote

In this lesson, you will learn how to style a block quote using two background images. The aim is to create a quotation that sits inside two large graphic quotation marks.

Applying the `<blockquote>` Element

The `<blockquote>` element is often used to indent text. However, it should not be used for this purpose. It should only be used to mark up long quotations that consist of block level content.

For this lesson, you will need a quotation and a source or author for the quotation. These two items will be marked up as paragraphs and then placed inside a `<blockquote>`. The paragraph that contains the source information will be given a `source` class. A class is used in this case because you might want to have more than one `<blockquote>` on a page.

Additional information about the source, such as a web address, can be added to the `<blockquote>` using the `cite` attribute as shown in Listing 13.1.

LISTING 13.1 HTML Code Containing the Markup for a Quotation

```
<blockquote cite="http://www.sitename.com/quote/smith.htm">
    <p>
        Lorem ipsum dolor ...
    </p>
    <p class="source">
        John  Smith
    </p>
</blockquote>
```

Semantically Correct Markup and Block Quotes
Semantically correct markup is about understanding HTML elements and what they mean. It is also about using these elements to give meaning to the content they contain.

If you use semantically correct markup, your content will have meaning in a wide range of devices, including text browsers, screen readers, and hand-held devices.

If you use poor semantic markup, however, your content will either have no meaning or incorrect meaning in a wide range of devices.

An example of poor semantic markup is using a <blockquote> to indent text. The <blockquote> will change the content presentation rather than add meaning. Even worse, the indented content is given incorrect meaning.

It would be far better to indent content using CSS and save the <blockquote> for its intended purpose—long quotations.

To style the <blockquote> and its content, you will use three selectors:

- The first is a type selector, used to target any instance of the <blockquote> on the page.

- The second is a descendant selector, used to target any <p> element inside a <blockquote>.

- The third is another descendant selector, used to target any <p> element that has been styled with the source class.

The selectors are shown in Listing 13.2.

LISTING 13.2   CSS Code Showing the Selectors for Styling the `<blockquote>`

```
blockquote {...}
blockquote p {...}
blockquote p.source {...}
```

Styling the `<blockquote>` Element

Unstyled `<blockquote>` elements are indented on the left and right sides. You can change this default behavior by resetting the margins. In this case, you will set the top and bottom margins to `1em` and the left and right margins to `0`. This can be achieved using a shorthand margin declaration—`margin: 1em 0`.

Next, you can apply a border to the `<blockquote>` to separate it from other content on the page. You can use a 1-pixel-wide border set to light gray, `border: 1px solid #ddd`.

The first background image will be applied directly to the `<blockquote>` element. The declaration will be `background-image: url(lesson13.gif)`.

The image will be positioned in the top left corner of the `<blockquote>`. This is achieved by setting the x and y axis to `5px` using a declaration of `background-position: 5px 5px`.

To stop the image from repeating across the entire `<blockquote>`, add `background-repeat: no-repeat`.

These three background declarations can be shortened into a single declaration using `background: url(lesson13.gif) 5px 5px no-repeat`. The background image is shown in Figure 13.1.

FIGURE 13.1   Background image applied to `<blockquote>`.

Now the image is in position, but the text is sitting over the top of it. This can be fixed by applying some padding to the top of the `<blockquote>`

using `padding-top: 30px` as shown in Listing 13.3. The results can be seen in Figure 13.2.

LISTING 13.3 CSS Code Styling the `<blockquote>`

```
blockquote
{
    margin: 1em 0;
    border: 1px solid #ddd;
    background: url(lesson13.gif) 5px 5px no-repeat;
    padding-top: 30px;
}
```

> Lorem ipsum dolor sit amet, consectetuer adipiscing elit, sed diam nonummy nibh euismod tincidunt ut laoreet dolore magna aliquam erat volutpat. Ut wisi enim ad minim veniam, quis nostrud exerci tation ullamcorper suscipit lobortis nisl ut aliquip ex ea commodo consequat. Duis autem vel eum iriure dolor in hendrerit in vulputate velit esse molestie consequat, vel illum dolore eu feugiat nulla facilisis at vero eros et accumsan et iusto odio dignissim qui blandit praesent luptatum zzril delenit augue duis dolore te feugait nulla facilisi.
>
> John Smith

FIGURE 13.2 Screenshot of styled `<blockquote>`.

Styling the Paragraph

Next, you will need to add padding to the left and right of any paragraphs inside the `<blockquote>`. This will push the content away from the borders. You can use `padding: 0 70px` as shown in Listing 13.4. The results can be seen in Figure 13.3.

LISTING 13.4 CSS Code Styling the Paragraph

```
blockquote
{
    margin: 1em 0;
    border: 1px solid #ddd;
```

LISTING 13.4   Continued

```
        background: url(lesson13.gif) 5px 5px no-repeat;
        padding-top: 30px;
}

blockquote p
{
        padding: 0 70px;
}
```

Lorem ipsum dolor sit amet,
consectetuer adipiscing elit, sed diam
nonummy nibh euismod tincidunt ut
laoreet dolore magna aliquam erat
volutpat. Ut wisi enim ad minim
veniam, quis nostrud exerci tation
ullamcorper suscipit lobortis nisl ut
aliquip ex ea commodo consequat.
Duis autem vel eum iriure dolor in
hendrerit in vulputate velit esse
molestie consequat, vel illum dolore
eu feugiat nulla facilisis at vero eros et
accumsan et iusto odio dignissim qui
blandit praesent luptatum zzril delenit
augue duis dolore te feugait nulla
facilisi.

John Smith

FIGURE 13.3   Screenshot of styled paragraph.

Styling the source Class

Now that the <blockquote> and paragraph elements are styled, you can
focus on the paragraph classed with source. This paragraph will be used
to place the second background image in the bottom-right corner of the
block quote.

A shorthand declaration can be used to set the image, repeat, and
position—background: url(lesson13a.gif) no-repeat 100% 100%.
The x and y axis must be set to 100% to place the bottom-right edge of the

image in the bottom-right corner of the paragraph. no-repeat should be
used to stop the image from repeating under the text. The background
image is shown in Figure 13.4.

Figure 13.4   Background image applied to paragraph classed
with source.

You will need to apply padding-bottom: 30px to the paragraph to push
the text up 30 pixels and stop it from sitting on top of the background
image.

The top image sits 5px in from the top and left edges of the
<blockquote>. To achieve the same result on the bottom, apply a 5px
margin to the right and bottom of the source class paragraph using
margin: 0 5px 5px 0.

Finally, the source text can be differentiated from other block quote text
by aligning it to the right and making it italic. This can be achieved with
text-align: right and font-style: italic as shown in Listing 13.5.
The results can be seen in Figure 13.5.

Listing 13.5   CSS Code Styling the source Class Paragraph

```
blockquote
{
    margin: 1em 0;
    border: 1px solid #ddd;
    background: url(lesson13.gif) 5px 5px no-repeat;
    padding-top: 30px;
}

blockquote p
{
    padding: 0 70px;
}

blockquote p.source
{
```

continues

LISTING 13.5   Continued

```
background: url(lesson13a.gif) no-repeat 100% 100%;
padding-bottom: 30px;
margin: 0 5px 5px 0;
text-align: right;
font-style: italic;
}
```

FIGURE 13.5   Screenshot of styled paragraph classed with source.

Creating a Variation

Using the same selectors and HTML code, it is possible to change the layout so that the `<blockquote>` and its content looks entirely different.

For this example, you will create a fixed-width `<blockquote>` with one large background image as shown in Figure 13.6.

FIGURE 13.6   Screenshot of new background image.

In the `blockquote` selector, the background image and its position need to change. In this case, both the x and y axes will be set to `0`, which means the image will sit in the top-left corner of the `<blockquote>`.

The `padding-top` declaration changes from `30px` to `1px` to trap paragraph margins.

Trapping Margins   A standard paragraph has predefined top and bottom margins.

When a paragraph is placed inside of another container, its top margin can cause problems. Some browsers will display the paragraph and top margin inside of the container. Other browsers, however, will display the paragraph only, and allow the margin to poke out the top of the container.

You can stop this from occurring by applying either `border-top` or `padding-top` to the container. The amount can be as tiny as 1px, as long as it is present.

This is referred to as trapping margins.

The `blockquote.p` selector changes from `padding: 0 70px` to `padding: 0 1em 0 80px`. This new padding will move the text away from the left edge of the `<blockquote>` to allow room for the new background image.

The `blockquote p.source` selector has a range of changes. The background image is removed completely. Margins are set to `0`. A `5px` white border is added to the top of the paragraph to separate the source from the quotation. Padding is changed from `padding-bottom: 30px` to `padding: .5em .5em .5em 80px`.

Finally, `text-align: right` is removed and `background: #336` is added. The results are shown in Listing 13.6. The results can be seen in Figure 13.7.

LISTING 13.6   CSS Code for the `<blockquote>` Variation

```
blockquote
{
    margin: 1em 0;
    border: 1px solid #000;
    background: #000 url(lesson13b.gif) no-repeat 0 0;
    padding-top: 1px;
    color: #fff;
    width: 500px;
}

blockquote p
{
    padding: 0 1em 0 80px;
}

blockquote p.source
{
    margin: 0;
    border-top: 5px solid #fff;
    padding: .5em .5em .5em 80px;
    background: #336;
    font-style: italic;
}
```

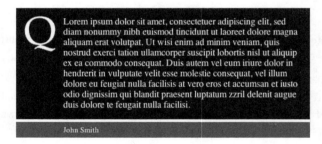

FIGURE 13.7   Screenshot of the `<blockquote>` variation.

Summary

In this lesson, you learned how to wrap the `<blockquote>` element around a long quotation and source, and then style it in different ways. In the next lesson, you will learn how to mark up and then style accessible data tables.

LESSON 14
Styling a Data Table

This lesson is divided into two sections. First, you will learn how to add accessibility features to a data table to make the content more accessible for screen readers. Second, you will learn how to style various elements within the table.

Starting with a Basic Table

As CSS increases in popularity, there is a growing trend to move away from using tables to mark up content. However, there are times when tables are the best markup option, especially for tabular data. A basic data table is shown in Listing 14.1.

LISTING 14.1 HTML Code Containing the Markup for a Data Table

```
<table>
    <tr>
        <td>Item</td>
        <td>Threaded screws </td>
        <td>Flat nails</td>
        <td>Dyna-bolts </td>
        <td>Spring washers</td>
    </tr>
    <tr>
        <td>1 kg</td>
        <td>$2.50</td>
        <td>$3.50</td>
        <td>$4.50</td>
        <td>$2.50</td>
    </tr>
    <tr>
```

continues

LISTING 14.1   Continued

```
        <td>2kg</td>
        <td>$3.00</td>
        <td>$4.00</td>
        <td>$5.00</td>
        <td>$3.00</td>
    </tr>
    <tr>
        <td>3kg</td>
        <td>$3.50</td>
        <td>$4.50</td>
        <td>$5.50</td>
        <td>$3.50</td>
    </tr>
    <tr>
        <td>4kg</td>
        <td>$4.00</td>
        <td>$5.00</td>
        <td>$6.00</td>
        <td>$4.00</td>
    </tr>
</table>
```

Adding Accessibility Features to a Data Table

There are a range of features that can be added to data tables to make them more accessible.

The summary attribute shown in Listing 14.2 should be used on complex data tables because it provides a clear description of what the table presents. It does not display on screens of current (standards-compliant) web browsers, but it can display on other web-browsing devices such as handhelds, cell phones, and so forth. The summary attribute is used as an orientation for people who use nonvisual devices.

LISTING 14.2   HTML Code Showing summary

```
<table summary="Table of screws, Flat nails, Dyna-bolts and
Spring washers, in kilos">
```

A caption should be included with any data table. It provides a brief description of the table's contents. Unlike the summary, the caption is displayed on the screen—usually centered above the table. The caption should appear directly after the opening table tag as shown in Listing 14.3.

LISTING 14.3   HTML Code Showing caption

```
<caption>
    Pricing for threaded screws, flat nails, dyna-bolts and
spring washers
</caption>
```

The <th> element, shown in Listing 14.4, should be used to define any row or column heading within a data table. It is used to create a relationship between <th> and <td> elements, which is important for nonvisual devices.

LISTING 14.4   HTML Code Showing <th> Elements

```
<th>Item</th>
<th>Threaded screws </th>
<th>Flat nails</th>
<th>Dyna-bolts </th>
<th>Spring washers</th>
```

The <thead>, <tbody>, and <tfoot> elements shown in Listing 14.5 are used to group rows in tables. The <thead> and <tfoot> should contain information about the table's columns and the <tbody> should contain the table data.

LISTING 14.5   HTML Showing <thead> and <tbody> Elements

```
<thead>
    <tr>
        <th>Item</th>
        <th>Threaded screws </th>
        <th>Flat nails</th>
        <th>Dyna-bolts </th>
        <th>Spring washers</th>
    </tr>
</thead>
<tbody>
```

continues

LISTING 14.5   Continued

```
<tr>
    <th>1 kg</th>
    <td>$2.50</td>
    <td>$3.50</td>
    <td>$4.50</td>
    <td>$2.50</td>
</tr>
</tbody>
```

The abbr attribute, shown in Listing 14.6, is used to provide an abbreviated form of the relevant cell's contents. The abbr attribute is important for people who use screen readers and may have to hear a cell's content read out loud repeatedly.

LISTING 14.6   HTML Code Showing abbr Attributes

```
<tr>
    <th>Item</th>
    <th abbr="screws">Threaded screws</th>
    <th abbr="nails">Flat nails</th>
    <th abbr="bolts">Dyna-bolts</th>
    <th abbr="washers">Spring washers</th>
</tr>
```

headers and ids are used to tie a table's data cells with their appropriate header. Each header must be given a unique id. The headers attribute is then added to each <td> element as shown in Listing 14.7.

LISTING 14.7   HTML Code Showing headers and ids

```
<table summary="Table of screws, Flat nails, Dyna-bolts and
Spring washers, in kilos">
    <caption>
        Pricing for threaded screws, flat nails, dyna-bolts
and spring washers
    </caption>
    <thead>
        <tr>
            <th>Item</th>
            <th id="screws" abbr="screws">Threaded
screws</th>
```

continues

```
            <th id="nails" abbr="nails">Flat nails</th>
            <th id="bolts" abbr="bolts">Dyna-bolts</th>
            <th id="washers" abbr="washers">Spring
            washers</th>
        </tr>
    </thead>
    <tbody>
        <tr>
            <th id="one">1 kg</th>
            <td headers="screws one">$2.50</td>
            <td headers="nails one">$3.50</td>
            <td headers="bolts one">$4.50</td>
            <td headers="washers one">$2.50</td>
        </tr>
        <tr>
            <th id="two">2kg</th>
            <td headers="screws two">$3.00</td>
            <td headers="nails two">$4.00</td>
            <td headers="bolts two">$5.00</td>
            <td headers="washers two">$3.00</td>
        </tr>
        <tr>
            <th id="three">3kg</th>
            <td headers="screws three">$3.50</td>
            <td headers="nails three">$4.50</td>
            <td headers="bolts three">$5.50</td>
            <td headers="washers three">$3.50</td>
        </tr>
        <tr>
            <th id="four">4kg</th>
            <td headers="screws four">$4.00</td>
            <td headers="nails four">$5.00</td>
            <td headers="bolts four">$6.00</td>
            <td headers="washers four">$4.00</td>
        </tr>
    </tbody>
</table>
```

Creating Selectors to Style a Table

To style this table and its content, you will use eight selectors as shown in Listing 14.8.

LISTING 14.8   CSS Code Showing the Selectors for Styling the Table

```
caption {...}
table {...}
th, td {...}
tr {...}
thead th {...}
tbody th {...}
tr.alternate {...}
tr.alternate th {...}
```

Styling the Caption

An unstyled table caption will be displayed above the table. On most modern browsers the caption will be center aligned, but you can change the default caption alignment using `text-align: left`.

To increase the space between the caption and its table, `margin-bottom` can be set to `.5em`.

The caption also can be given more weight to make it stand out from the table content. This is achieved using `font-weight:bold` as shown in Listing 14.9. The results can be seen in Figure 14.1.

LISTING 14.9   CSS Code for Styling the Caption

```
caption
{
    text-align: left;
    margin: 0 0 .5em 0;
    font-weight: bold;
}
```

Pricing for threaded screws, flat nails, dyna-bolts and spring washers			
Item Threaded screws Flat nails Dyna-bolts Spring washers			
1 kg $2.50	$3.50	$4.50	$2.50
2kg $3.00	$4.00	$5.00	$3.00
3kg $3.50	$4.50	$5.50	$3.50
4kg $4.00	$5.00	$6.00	$4.00

FIGURE 14.1   Screenshot of styled caption.

Styling the `<table>` Element

Apply `border-collapse: collapse` to the `<table>` element to remove cellspacing as shown in Listing 14.10.

LISTING 14.10   CSS Code for Styling the `<table>` Element

```
caption
{
    text-align: left;
    margin: 0 0 .5em 0;
    font-weight: bold;
}

table
{
    border-collapse: collapse;
}
```

> **Tables and cellspacing**   A standard table will have about 2px of `cellspacing` between cells. This can be removed using two methods.
>
> The first method is to apply `cellspacing="0"` as an attribute inside the `<table>` element. This is not ideal because a presentation attribute has been added to the table. If you were to change the presentation at a later date, you would need to adjust the HTML as well as the CSS.
>
> The second method is to apply `border-collapse: collapse` to the `<table>` element using CSS. This method is preferred because the appearance of the table can be changed at any time without affecting the HTML.

Styling the `<th>` and `<td>` Elements

Now the `<th>` and `<td>` elements need to be styled with a right and bottom border. Because the border will appear on all `<td>` and `<th>` elements, you can group both elements into one selector.

Applying a border is more powerful than using `cellspacing` because you can change the color or width of these borders at any time to suit your needs.

To apply padding to all cells, use `padding:   .5em` as shown in Listing 14.11.

LISTING 14.11   CSS Code for Styling the <th> and <td> Elements

```
caption
{
    text-align: left;
    margin: 0 0 .5em 0;
    font-weight: bold;
}

table
{
    border-collapse: collapse;
}

th, td
{
    border-right: 1px solid #fff;
    border-bottom: 1px solid #fff;
    padding: .5em;
}
```

Styling the <tr> Element

The <tr> element should be styled with a `background-color` as shown in Listing 14.12. This color can be changed to suit your needs. The results can be seen in Figure 14.2.

LISTING 14.12   CSS Code for Styling the <tr> Element

```
caption
{
    text-align: left;
    margin: 0 0 .5em 0;
    font-weight: bold;
}
```

```
table
{
        border-collapse: collapse;
}

th, td
{
    border-right: 1px solid #fff;
    border-bottom: 1px solid #fff;
    padding: .5em;
}

tr
{
    background: #B0C4D7;
}
```

Pricing for threaded screws, flat nails, dyna-bolts and spring washers				
Item	**Threaded screws**	**Flat nails**	**Dyna-bolts**	**Spring washers**
1 kg	$2.50	$3.50	$4.50	$2.50
2kg	$3.00	$4.00	$5.00	$3.00
3kg	$3.50	$4.50	$5.50	$3.50
4kg	$4.00	$5.00	$6.00	$4.00

FIGURE 14.2   Screenshot of styled <tr> element.

Targeting Instances of the <th> Element

The next step is to create background colors for the <th> element. Using descendant selectors, it is possible to apply different colors to the <th> elements on the top and left side of the table.

The <th> elements across the top of the table are styled with thead th {...} because they appear inside the <thead> element.

The <th> elements down the side of the table are styled with tbody th {...} because they appear inside the <tbody> element.

The <th> elements down the side also can be set to font-weight: normal to differentiate them from the headers across the top as shown in Listing 14.13. The results can be seen in Figure 14.3.

LISTING 14.13   CSS Code for Styling the <th> Elements

```
caption
{
    text-align: left;
    margin: 0 0 .5em 0;
    font-weight: bold;
}

table
{
    border-collapse: collapse;
}

th, td
{
    border-right: 1px solid #fff;
    border-bottom: 1px solid #fff;
    padding: .5em;
}

tr
{
    background: #B0C4D7;
}

thead th
{
    background: #036;
    color: #fff;
}

tbody th
{
    font-weight: normal;
    background: #658CB1;
}
```

Figure 14.3 Screenshot of styled `<th>` elements.

Creating Alternate Row Colors

It is possible to style alternate table rows so that they have different background colors. This aids readability, especially on a long table.

One method is to add a class to every second `<tr>` element. In this case, the class is `alternate`. The `<td>` and `<th>` elements within these rows can be given a slightly different background color. The selectors will need to be `tr.alternate td {...}` and `tr.alternate th {..}` as shown in Listing 14.14. The results can be seen in Figure 14.4.

LISTING 14.14 CSS Code for Styling Alternate Rows

```
caption
{
    text-align: left;
    margin: 0 0 .5em 0;
    font-weight: bold;
}

table
{
    border-collapse: collapse;
}

th, td
{
    border-right: 1px solid #fff;
    border-bottom: 1px solid #fff;
```

LISTING 14.14   Continued

```
    padding: .5em;
}

tr
{
    background: #B0C4D7;
}

thead th
{
    background: #036;
    color: #fff;
}

tbody th
{
    font-weight: normal;
    background: #658CB1;
}

tr.alternate
{
    background: #D7E0EA;
}

tr.alternate th
{
    background: #8AA9C7;
}
```

Pricing for threaded screws, flat nails, dyna-bolts and spring washers				
Item	Threaded screws	Flat nails	Dyna-bolts	Spring washers
1 kg	$2.50	$3.50	$4.50	$2.50
2kg	$3.00	$4.00	$5.00	$3.00
3kg	$3.50	$4.50	$5.50	$3.50
4kg	$4.00	$5.00	$6.00	$4.00

FIGURE 14.4   Screenshot of styled alternate rows.

Summary

In this lesson, you learned how to add accessibility features to a data table, including summary, caption, <thead>, <th>, headers, and ids. You also learned how to style the table and its elements. These accessibility features not only enhance the website via other devices, but help create CSS suitable for these devices. In the next lesson, you will learn how to create vertical navigation.

LESSON 15
Creating Vertical Navigation

In this lesson, you will learn how to create vertical navigation. You will also learn how to apply background images and hover effects.

Why Use a List?

At its most basic level, site navigation is simply a list of links to other pages in the site. So, a standard HTML list is the ideal starting point (see Listing 15.1). The resulting list is shown in Figure 15.1.

LISTING 15.1 HTML Code Containing the Markup for a List

```
<ul id="navigation">
    <li><a href="#">Home</a></li>
    <li><a href="#">About</a></li>
    <li><a href="#">Services</a></li>
    <li><a href="#">Staff</a></li>
    <li><a href="#">Portfolio</a></li>
    <li><a href="#">Contact</a></li>
    <li><a href="#">Sitemap</a></li>
</ul>
```

- Home
- About
- Services
- Staff
- Portfolio
- Contact
- Sitemap

FIGURE 15.1 Screenshot of unstyled list.

Styling the List

To style this list, you will need to use selectors that target the `<ul>`, `<li>`, and `<a>` elements. To make sure you do not target every instance of these elements on the page, you will need to include the unique identifier, `navigation`, within each selector. The four selectors that you will use are shown in Listing 15.2.

LISTING 15.2   CSS Code Showing the Selectors for Styling the List

```
ul#navigation {...}
ul#navigation a {...}
ul#navigation a:hover {...}
ul#navigation li {...}
```

 What Are Selectors? Selectors are used to "select" elements on an HTML page so that they can be styled.

For more information, see Lesson 3, "Selectors in Action."

Styling the `<ul>` Element

Most browsers display HTML lists with left indentation. To set this indentation, some browsers use padding (Firefox, Netscape, and Safari), and others use margins (Internet Explorer and Opera).

To remove this left indentation consistently across all browsers, set both `padding-left` and `margin-left` to 0 on the `<ul>` element as shown in Listing 15.3.

LISTING 15.3   CSS Code for Zeroing Margins and Padding

```
ul#navigation
{
    margin-left: 0;
    padding-left: 0;
}
```

To remove the list bullets, set the `list-style-type` to none as in Listing 15.4. The results of the CSS style rules are shown in Figure 15.2.

LISTING 15.4   CSS Code for Removing List Bullets

```
ul#navigation
{
    margin-left: 0;
    padding-left: 0;
    list-style-type: none;
}
```

> Home
> About
> Services
> Staff
> Portfolio
> Contact
> Sitemap

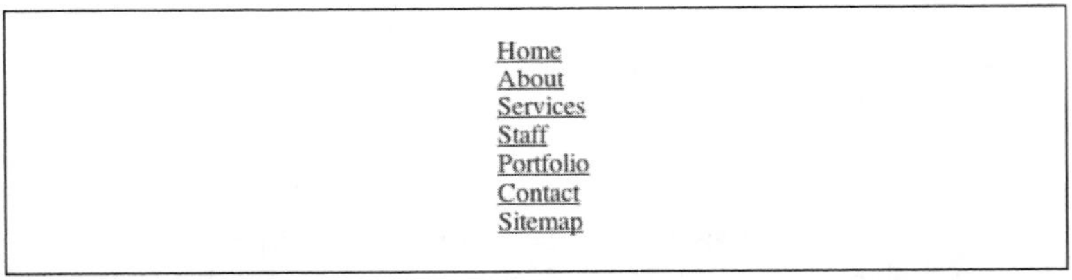

FIGURE 15.2   Screenshot of list with the `<ul>` element styled.

Styling the `<a>` Element

Text links are generally only active when you mouse over the actual text area. You can increase this active area by applying `display: block;` to the `<a>` element. This will change it from inline to block level, and the active area will extend to the full width of the list item.

When the `<a>` element is block level, users do not have to click on the text; they can click on any area of the list item.

Style the `<a>` elements with `display: block;` as shown in Listing 15.5.

LISTING 15.5   CSS Code for Setting `display: block`

```
ul#navigation
{
    margin-left: 0;
    padding-left: 0;
    list-style-type: none;
}
```

continues

```
ul#navigation a
{
    display: block;
}
```

To remove the underlines on the links, use `text-decoration: none;` (see Listing 15.6).

LISTING 15.6   CSS Code for Removing Link Underlining

```
ul#navigation
{
    margin-left: 0;
    padding-left: 0;
    list-style-type: none;
}

ul#navigation a
{
    display: block;
    text-decoration: none;
}
```

Changing Link Behavior   Changing standard hyperlink behavior (such as removing underlines) can be confusing for some users who might not realize that the item is a link.

For this reason, it is generally not a good idea to remove underlines on links unless you provide some other means to allow users to distinguish links.

To set the background color, you can use the shorthand rule `background: #036;` as shown in Listing 15.7. This color can be changed to suit your needs.

LISTING 15.7   CSS Code for Setting Background Color

```
ul#navigation
{
    margin-left: 0;
    padding-left: 0;
    list-style-type: none;
}

ul#navigation a
{
    display: block;
    text-decoration: none;
    background: #036;
}
```

Next, the text color should be set to #fff (the hex color for white). See Listing 15.8. Like the background color, text color can be changed to suit your needs.

LISTING 15.8   CSS Code for Setting Text Color

```
ul#navigation
{
    margin-left: 0;
    padding-left: 0;
    list-style-type: none;
}

ul#navigation a
{
    display: block;
    text-decoration: none;
    background: #036;
    color: #fff;
}
```

You will need .2em padding on the top and bottom of the <a> element, and .5em padding on both sides. Rather than specify these amounts in separate declarations, you can use one shorthand declaration to define them all. In this case you will use padding: .2em .5em, which will apply .2em of padding on the top and bottom of the <a> element, and .5em on both sides as shown in Listing 15.9.

LISTING 15.9   CSS Code for Setting Padding

```
ul#navigation
{
    margin-left: 0;
    padding-left: 0;
    list-style-type: none;
}

ul#navigation a
{
    display: block;
    text-decoration: none;
    background: #036;
    color: #fff;
    padding: .2em .5em;
}
```

 Why Use Ems? You can use either pixels or ems to specify measurement units for padding, margins, and widths. Ems are more flexible because they scale up or down to match the user's font size settings.

To provide some space between the list items, you can add a border on the bottom of each list item. In this case you will use `border-bottom: #fff` as shown in Listing 15.10.

LISTING 15.10   CSS Code for Setting Borders

```
ul#navigation
{
    margin-left: 0;
    padding-left: 0;
    list-style-type: none;
}

ul#navigation a
{
    display: block;
    text-decoration: none;
    background: #036;
```

continues

LISTING 15.10   Continued

```
    color: #fff;
    padding: .2em .5em;
    border-bottom: 1px solid #fff;
}
```

Customizing the Border Bottom   In this lesson, the border-bottom is set to #fff, assuming that the page background is white. However, the color of the border-bottom should be set in the same color as the page or container background.

If more space is required between list items, the width of the border can be increased.

Set the width of the <a> element using width: 7em; as shown in Listing 15.11 and illustrated in Figure 15.3. This width can be changed to suit your needs.

LISTING 15.11   CSS Code for Setting Width

```
ul#navigation
{
    margin-left: 0;
    padding-left: 0;
    list-style-type: none;
}

ul#navigation a
{
    display: block;
    text-decoration: none;
    background: #036;
    color: #fff;
    padding: .2em .5em;
    border-bottom: 1px solid #fff;
    width: 7em;
}
```

List Width   As discussed in Lesson 5, "Getting to Know the CSS Box Model," padding is added to the content area to give a final width. In this case, .5em of padding is applied to the left and right sides of the list. When added to the content width of 7em, the list items are now 8em wide.

FIGURE 15.3   Screenshot of list with <a> element styled.

 Fixing Odd Borders   Certain browsers, such as Netscape, Mozilla, and Firefox, will render the border-bottom incorrectly for some list items—generally in the middle of a list. This can be fixed by changing the border thickness to 1em instead of 1px.

Adding a Hover Effect

The :hover pseudo-class can be used to change the style of links when they are rolled over. In this case, you will set the background to #69C and the color to #000 as shown in Listing 15.12. The results can be seen in Figure 15.4. These colors can be changed to suit your needs.

LISTING 15.12   CSS Code for Setting Hover

```
ul#navigation
{
    margin-left: 0;
    padding-left: 0;
    list-style-type: none;
}

ul#navigation a
{
    display: block;
    text-decoration: none;
    background: #036;
    color: #fff;
    padding: .2em .5em;
    border-bottom: 1px solid #fff;
    width: 7em;
}

ul#navigation a:hover
{
    background: #69C;
    color: #000;
}
```

FIGURE 15.4   Screenshot of list showing hover.

Styling the `<li>` Element

You might notice that there are slight gaps between list items in some versions of Internet Explorer for Windows or Opera. This can be overcome by setting the `<li>` element to `display: inline` (see Listing 15.13).

LISTING 15.13   CSS Code for Setting `display: Inline` on the `<li>` Element

```
ul#navigation
{
    margin-left: 0;
    padding-left: 0;
    list-style-type: none;
}

ul#navigation a
{
    display: block;
    text-decoration: none;
    background: #036;
    color: #fff;
    padding: .2em .5em;
    border-bottom: 1px solid #fff;
    width: 7em;
}

ul#navigation a:hover
{
    background: #69C;
    color: #000;
}

ul#navigation li
{
    display: inline;
}
```

Summary

In this lesson, you have learned that lists can be styled to look like a vertical navigation panel, how to set declarations on the <a> element, and how to use the :hover pseudo-class. In the next lesson, you will learn how to create horizontal navigation.

LESSON 16

Creating Horizontal Navigation

In this lesson, you will learn how to create horizontal navigation from a standard HTML list. You will also learn how to float the <ul> element to create a navigation bar and float the <a> element to create a series of square buttons—each with a thin dividing line down its right edge.

Styling the List

To style this list, you will need to use selectors that target the <ul>, <li>, and <a> elements. You will also need to include the unique identifier, navigation, within each selector. The four selectors that you will use are shown in Listing 16.1. The HTML code is shown in Listing 16.2.

LISTING 16.1   CSS Code Showing the Selectors for Styling the List

```
ul#navigation {...}
ul#navigation li {...}
ul#navigation a {...}
ul#navigation a:hover {...}
```

LISTING 16.2   HTML Code Containing the Markup for a List

```
<ul id="navigation">
    <li><a href="#">Home</a></li>
    <li><a href="#">About</a></li>
    <li><a href="#">Services</a></li>
    <li><a href="#">Staff</a></li>
    <li><a href="#">Portfolio</a></li>
    <li><a href="#">Contact</a></li>
</ul>
```

Styling the `<ul>` Element

As discussed in Lesson 15, "Creating Vertical Navigation," most browsers display HTML lists with left indentation. To remove this left indentation, set both `padding-left` and `margin-left` to `0` on the `<ul>` element as shown in Listing 16.3.

LISTING 16.3   CSS Code Zeroing Margins and Padding

```
ul#navigation
{
    margin-left: 0;
    padding-left: 0;
}
```

To remove the list bullets, set the `list-style-type` to `none` as in Listing 16.4.

LISTING 16.4   CSS Code Removing List Bullets

```
ul#navigation
{
    margin-left: 0;
    padding-left: 0;
    list-style-type: none;
}
```

Next, add a background color using the shorthand `background: #036;` as shown in Listing 16.5. This color can be changed to suit your needs.

LISTING 16.5   CSS Code Setting Background Color

```
ul#navigation
{
    margin-left: 0;
    padding-left: 0;
    list-style-type: none;
    background: #036;
}
```

To float the `<ul>`, use `float: left`. You will also need to set a width. In this case, we will use `100%` because we want the list to spread across the full width of the page. The results are shown in Listing 16.6 and illustrated in Figure 16.1. At this stage, the text is almost illegible. This will be addressed when the `<a>` element is styled.

Why Float the `<ul>` and `<a>` Elements?   In this lesson, both the `<ul>` and `<a>` elements need to be floated.

The `<a>` element is floated so that the list items sit in a horizontal line, butting up against each other.

The `<ul>` must be floated so that it wraps around the `<a>` elements. Otherwise, it will have no height and will not be visible.

LISTING 16.6   CSS Code Setting Float and Width

```
ul#navigation
{
    margin-left: 0;
    padding-left: 0;
    list-style-type: none;
    background: #036;
    float: left;
    width: 100%;
}
```

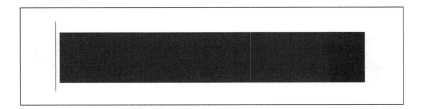

FIGURE 16.1   Screenshot of list with the `<ul>` element styled.

Styling the `<li>` Element

To make sure the list items are displayed in a single line, the `<li>` element must be set to `display: inline` as shown in Listing 16.7. The results can be seen in Figure 16.2.

Listing 16.7 CSS Code Setting `display: inline;`

```
ul#navigation
{
    margin-left: 0;
    padding-left: 0;
    list-style-type: none;
    background: #036;
    float: left;
    width: 100%;
}

ul#navigation li
{
    display: inline;
}
```

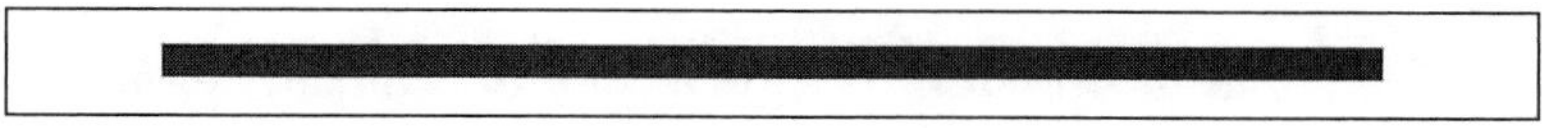

FIGURE 16.2 Screenshot of list with the `<li>` element styled.

Styling the `<a>` Element

You can increase the active area of text links by applying `display: block;` to the `<a>` element. This will change it from inline to block level and allow you to apply padding to all sides of the element.

Set the `<a>` element to `display: block;` so that padding can be applied to all sides. This will give the element additional width and height, increasing the clickable area.

The `<a>` element should then be floated, so that each list item moves into a single line butting against the previous item (see Listing 16.8).

Listing 16.8 CSS Code Setting `display: block;`

```
ul#navigation
{
    margin-left: 0;
    padding-left: 0;
    list-style-type: none;
    background: #036;
```

continues

Listing 16.8 Continued

```
        float: left;
        width: 100%;
}

ul#navigation li
{
        display: inline;
}

ul#navigation a
{
        display: block;
        float: left;
}
```

Floats and Width   For this lesson, you will not be setting a width on the floated <a> elements. This will
allow each list item to have its own width based on
the number of characters and the surrounding
padding.

However, this is not generally considered to be a good
practice. It is best to set a width on all floated items
(except if applied directly to an image, which has
implicit width).

If no width is set, the results can be unpredictable.
Theoretically, a floated element with an undefined
width should shrink to the widest element within it.
This could be a word, a sentence, or even a single
character—and results can vary from browser to
browser.

In this case, the results are acceptable because the
styled list displays well in almost all modern browsers
(including Internet Explore 5+, Netscape 6+, Opera 6+,
Firefox, and Safari).

Next, add some padding using the `padding` declaration. You can use `.2em` for top and bottom padding, and `1em` for left and right padding as shown in Listing 16.9.

LISTING 16.9   CSS Code Setting Padding

```
ul#navigation
{
    margin-left: 0;
    padding-left: 0;
    list-style-type: none;
    background: #036;
    float: left;
    width: 100%;
}

ul#navigation li
{
    display: inline;
}

ul#navigation a
{
    display: block;
    float: left;
    padding: .2em 1em;
}
```

To remove the underlines on the links, use `text-decoration: none;`. To set the text color and background color, use `color:  #fff;` (white) and `background: #036;` as shown in Listing 16.10. These colors can be changed to suit your needs.

LISTING 16.10   CSS Code Setting Text Decoration, Color, and Background Color

```
ul#navigation
{
    margin-left: 0;
    padding-left: 0;
    list-style-type: none;
    background: #036;
    float: left;
    width: 100%;
}
```

continues

LISTING 16.10   Continued

```
ul#navigation li
{
    display: inline;
}

ul#navigation a
{
    display: block;
    float: left;
    padding: .2em 1em;
    text-decoration: none;
    color: #fff;
    background: #036;
}
```

To separate each list item, a white line divider will be added to the end of each item. This is achieved by adding a white border to the right side of each list item, using `border-right: 1px solid #fff;` as shown in Listing 16.11 and illustrated in Figure 16.3.

LISTING 16.11   CSS Code Setting a Border

```
ul#navigation
{
    margin-left: 0;
    padding-left: 0;
    list-style-type: none;
    background: #036;
    float: left;
    width: 100%;
}

ul#navigation li
{
    display: inline;
}

ul#navigation a
{
    display: block;
    float: left;
    padding: .2em 1em;
    text-decoration: none;
```

continues

```
    color: #fff;
    background: #036;
    border-right: 1px solid #fff;
}
```

FIGURE 16.3   Screenshot of list with the <a> element styled.

Styling the :hover Pseudo Class

Finally, the :hover pseudo class is used to change the style of links when they are rolled over. In this case, you will set the background to #69C and the color to #000 as shown in Listing 16.12 and illustrated in Figure 16.4. These colors can be changed to suit your needs.

LISTING 16.12   CSS Code Setting a Hover

```
ul#navigation
{
    margin-left: 0;
    padding-left: 0;
    list-style-type: none;
    background: #036;
    float: left;
    width: 100%;
}

ul#navigation li
{
    display: inline;
}

ul#navigation a
{
    display: block;
    float: left;
    padding: .2em 1em;
    text-decoration: none;
    color: #fff;
    background: #036;
```

continues

LISTING 16.12   Continued

```
    border-right: 1px solid #fff;
}

ul#navigation a:hover
{
    color: #000;
    background: #69C;
}
```

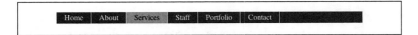

FIGURE 16.4   Screenshot of finished list.

Summary

In this lesson you have learned that lists can be styled to look like a horizontal navigation panel, how to float the <ul> and <a> elements, and how to use the :hover pseudo class. In the next lesson, you will learn how to style a round-cornered box.

LESSON 17
Styling a Round-Cornered Box

In this lesson, you will learn how to create a flexible-width, round-cornered box using four corner images.

Setting Up the HTML Code

The HTML code for this lesson is comprised of an overall `<div>` container, a heading, and two paragraphs. The `<div>` is styled with a `pullquote` id, and the second paragraph is styled with a `furtherinfo` class as shown in Listing 17.1.

LISTING 17.1 HTML Code Containing the Markup for a Round-Cornered Box

```
<div id="pullquote">
    <h2>Heading here</h2>
    <p>
        Lorem ipsum dolor sit amet....
    </p>
    <p class="furtherinfo">
        <a href="#">More information</a>
    </p>
</div>
```

Creating the Illusion of Round Corners

There are many methods that can be used to create a flexible-width, round-cornered box. The method described in this lesson uses four individual corner images.

These images should not be placed in the HTML code because they are purely presentational. Ideally, they should be applied as background images using CSS.

The top-left image will be applied as a background image to the <div> container and the top-right image will be applied to the <h2> element.

The bottom-left image will be applied to the last <p> element inside the box. This <p> element will be given a .furtherinfo class to differentiate it from other paragraphs in the box.

The bottom-right image will be applied to a specific instance of the <a> element.

 Adding Elements to Achieve Round Corners   There are many ways to create a flexible-width, round-cornered box.

One commonly used method involves nesting four levels of <div> elements that are then used to position the background images.

Where possible, it is better to use existing HTML elements or instances of elements rather than add new elements. Additional elements create unnecessary markup, which can increase page size and make maintenance more difficult.

Creating Selectors to Style the Round-Cornered Box

To style the round-cornered box, you will need to use the five selectors shown in Listing 17.2.

LISTING 17.2   CSS Code Showing the Selectors for Styling the Two-Column Layout

```
div#pullquote
div#pullquote h2
```

```
div#pullquote p
div#pullquote p.furtherinfo
div#pullquote p.furtherinfo a
```

Preparing the Images

The four images used in this lesson are shown in Figures 17.1 through 17.4. The style and color of these images can be changed to suit your needs.

FIGURE 17.1 Image 1, which will be applied to the `<div>` element. The image should be made over 2,000 pixels long so that it will grow to the width of the widest monitors.

FIGURE 17.2 Image 2, which will be applied to the `<h2>` element.

FIGURE 17.3 Image 3, which will be applied to the `<p>` element styled with `.furtherinfo`.

FIGURE 17.4 Image 4, which will be applied to the `<a>` element.

Styling the `<div>` Element

The first step in creating a round-cornered box is to style the `<div>`, which needs to be given some space on all sides. This can be achieved using `margin: 2em`. Next, the `<div>` needs to have a background image applied to the top-left corner. Use `background: #09f url(lesson17a.gif) no-repeat;` as shown in Listing 17.3. The results can be seen in Figure 17.5.

LISTING 17.3   CSS Code for Styling the `<div>` Element

```
div#pullquote
{
    margin: 2em;
    background: #09f url(lesson17a.gif) no-repeat;
}
```

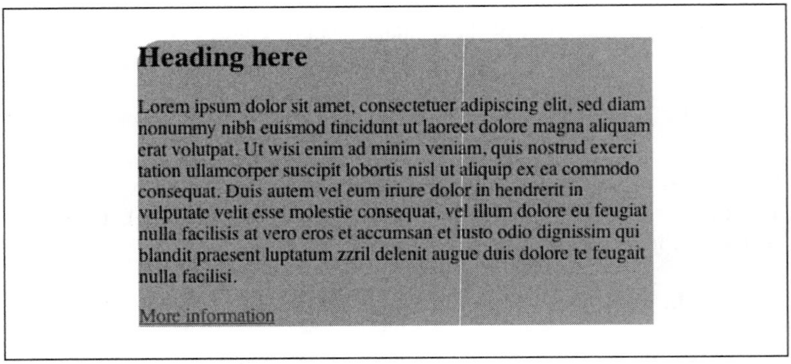

FIGURE 17.5   Screenshot of styled `<div>` element.

Styling the `<h2>` Element

Now that the `<div>` has been styled, the `<h2>` element will be used to position the second background image in the top-right corner.

The `<h2>` element's margins have to be turned off using `margin: 0`.

Next, the `<h2>` needs some padding on all edges except the bottom. This is achieved using `padding: 20px 20px 0 20px`.

Finally, the background image is added using `background: url (lesson17b.gif) no-repeat 100% 0;`. The horizontal background position is set to `100%`, so the right edge of the image will sit against the right edge of the `<h2>` element. The image is also set to `no-repeat` so that it does not repeat across the background of the `<h2>` element as shown in Listing 17.4. The results can be seen in Figure 17.6.

Listing 17.4   CSS Code for Styling the `<div>` Element

```
div#pullquote
{
    margin: 2em;
    background: #09f url(lesson17a.gif) no-repeat;
}

div#pullquote h2
{
    margin: 0;
    padding: 20px 20px 0 20px;
    background: url(lesson17b.gif) no-repeat 100% 0;
}
```

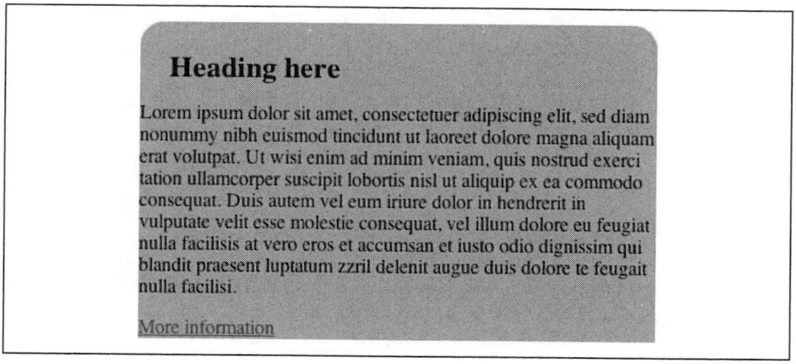

Heading here

Lorem ipsum dolor sit amet, consectetuer adipiscing elit, sed diam nonummy nibh euismod tincidunt ut laoreet dolore magna aliquam erat volutpat. Ut wisi enim ad minim veniam, quis nostrud exerci tation ullamcorper suscipit lobortis nisl ut aliquip ex ea commodo consequat. Duis autem vel eum iriure dolor in hendrerit in vulputate velit esse molestie consequat, vel illum dolore eu feugiat nulla facilisis at vero eros et accumsan et iusto odio dignissim qui blandit praesent luptatum zzril delenit augue duis dolore te feugait nulla facilisi.

More information

FIGURE 17.6   Screenshot of styled `<h2>` element.

Styling the `<p>` Element

The `<p>` element must be padded on both sides to keep it away from the edges of its container. This can be achieved using `padding: 0 20px` as shown in Listing 17.5. The results can be seen in Figure 17.7.

Listing 17.5   CSS Code for Styling the `<p>` Element

```
div#pullquote
{
    margin: 2em;
    background: #09f url(lesson17a.gif) no-repeat;
}
```

continues

Listing 17.5   Continued

```
div#pullquote h2
{
    margin: 0;
    padding: 20px 20px 0 20px;
    background: url(lesson17b.gif) no-repeat 100% 0;
}

div#pullquote p
{
    padding: 0 20px;
}
```

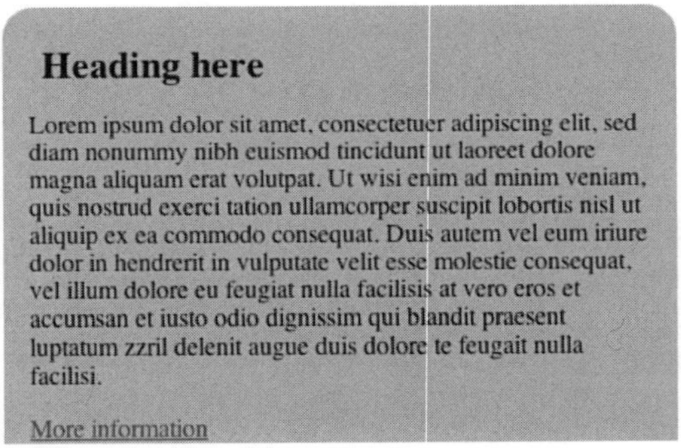

Figure 17.7   Screenshot of styled <p> element.

Styling the .furtherinfo Class

The last paragraph inside the round-cornered box is styled with a
.furtherinfo class. This paragraph will be used to position the third
image in the bottom-left corner.

The paragraph must be given some padding, but it will only be padded on
the left edge. This can be achieved using padding: 0 0 0 20px.

The background image can be set using background:
url(lesson17c.gif) no-repeat 0 100%;. The vertical background position is set to 100%, so the bottom edge of the image will sit against the
bottom of the <p> element. The image is also set to no-repeat so that it

does not repeat across the background of the <p> element as shown in Listing 17.6. The results can be seen in Figure 17.8.

LISTING 17.6   CSS Code for Styling the `.furtherinfo` Class

```
div#pullquote
{
    margin: 2em;
    background: #09f url(lesson17a.gif) no-repeat;
}

div#pullquote h2
{
    margin: 0;
    padding: 20px 20px 0 20px;
    background: url(lesson17b.gif) no-repeat 100% 0;
}

div#pullquote p
{
    padding: 0 20px;
}

div#pullquote p.furtherinfo
{
    padding: 0 0 0 20px;
    background: url(lesson17c.gif) no-repeat 0 100%;
}
```

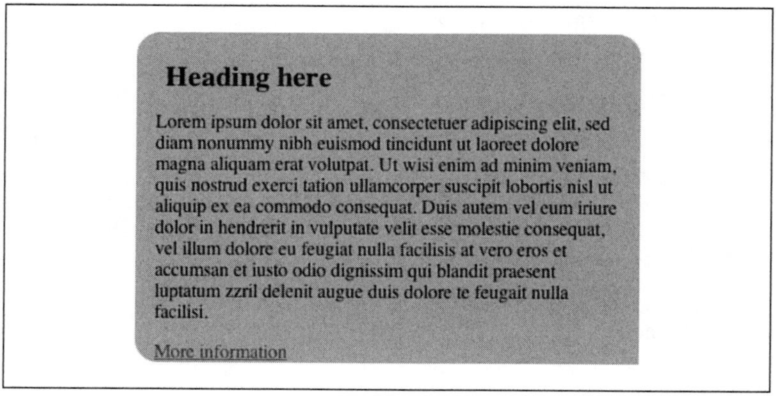

Figure 17.8   Screenshot of styled `.furtherinfo` class.

Styling the \<a> Element

The bottom-right image is applied to the \<a> element.

In order for the image to display correctly, the \<a> element must first be converted to block level using display: block.

The next step is to add padding using padding: 0 20px 20px 0;. This will apply padding to the right and bottom of the element.

The content of the \<a> element can be aligned to the right by using text-align: right.

Finally, the background image is applied using background: url (lesson17d.gif) no-repeat 100% 100%; as shown in Listing 17.7. This will apply the image to the bottom-right edge of the \<a> element. The results can be seen in Figure 17.9.

LISTING 17.7   CSS Code for Styling the \<a> Element

```
div#pullquote
{
    margin: 2em;
    background: #09f url(lesson17a.gif) no-repeat;
}

div#pullquote h2
{
    margin: 0;
    padding: 20px 20px 0 20px;
    background: url(lesson17b.gif) no-repeat 100% 0;
}

div#pullquote p
{
    padding: 0 20px;
}

div#pullquote p.furtherinfo
{
    padding: 0 0 0 20px;
    background: url(lesson17c.gif) no-repeat 0 100%;
}

div#pullquote p.furtherinfo a
```

continues

```
{
    display: block;
    padding: 0 20px 20px 0;
    text-align: right;
    background: url(lesson17d.gif) no-repeat 100% 100%;
}
```

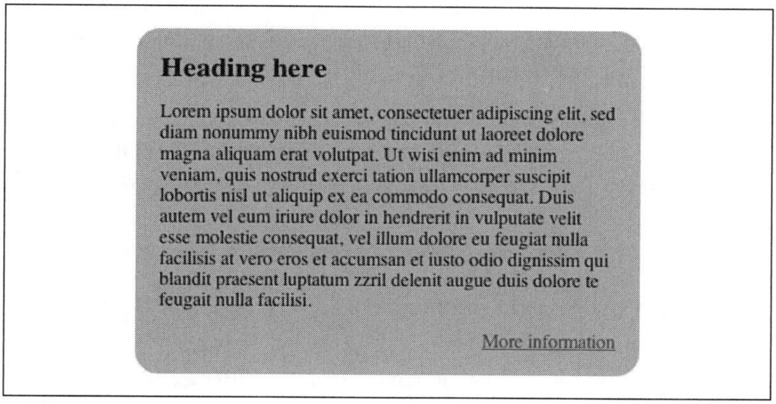

Heading here

Lorem ipsum dolor sit amet, consectetuer adipiscing elit, sed diam nonummy nibh euismod tincidunt ut laoreet dolore magna aliquam erat volutpat. Ut wisi enim ad minim veniam, quis nostrud exerci tation ullamcorper suscipit lobortis nisl ut aliquip ex ea commodo consequat. Duis autem vel eum iriure dolor in hendrerit in vulputate velit esse molestie consequat, vel illum dolore eu feugiat nulla facilisis at vero eros et accumsan et iusto odio dignissim qui blandit praesent luptatum zzril delenit augue duis dolore te feugait nulla facilisi.

More information

FIGURE 17.9   Screenshot of styled <a> element.

Creating a Fixed-Width Variation

Creating a fixed-width version of the round-cornered box requires only two background images.

The first image can be applied to the <div> container using `background: #09f url(lesson17f.gif) no-repeat 0 100%;`. This will place the image in the bottom corner of the box. The image used is shown in Figure 17.10.

FIGURE 17.10   Background image used to style the <div> element.

The <div> element needs to be given a width to match the width of the two images. `400px` has been used here. This measurement can be changed to suit your needs.

The `<div>` must also be given some bottom padding so that the text doesn't sit over the top of the image. This can be achieved using `padding-bottom: 20px`.

The `<p>` element must be padded on both sides to keep it away from the edges of its container. This can be achieved using `padding: 0 20px`.

The `<h2>` element must have the margins set to `0` so that there are no gaps at the top of the container. It must also be padded on the top right and left using `padding: 20px 20px 0 20px;`.

A background image is applied to the `<h2>` element using `background: url(lesson17e.gif) no-repeat 100% 0;`. This will position the image at the top left of the element. The image is shown in Figure 17.11.

Figure 17.11   Background image used to style the `<h2>` element.

Finally, the `.furtherinfo` paragraph content needs to be aligned right. This can be achieved using `text-align: right` as shown in Listing 17.8. The results can be seen in Figure 17.12.

Listing 17.8   CSS Code for Styling the Fixed-Width, Round-Cornered Box

```
div#pullquote
{
    background: #09f url(lesson17f.gif) no-repeat 0 100%;
    width: 400px;
    padding-bottom: 20px;
}

div#pullquote p
{
    padding: 0 20px;
}

div#pullquote h2
{
    margin: 0;
    padding: 20px 20px 0 20px;
    background: url(lesson17e.gif) no-repeat 100% 0;
}
```

continues

```
div#pullquote p.furtherinfo
{
    text-align: right;
}
```

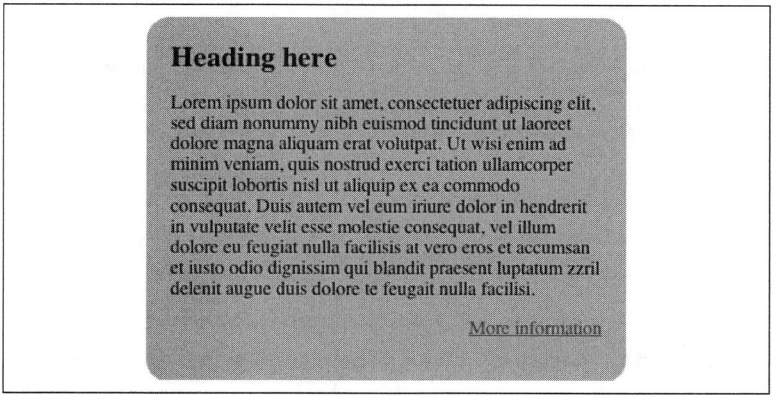

Figure 17.12   Screenshot of fixed-width, round-cornered box.

Creating a Top-Only Flexible Variation

To create a top-only flexible variation of the round-cornered box, two background images are needed.

The first image can be applied to the `<div>` container using `background: #fff url(lesson17g.jpg) no-repeat;`. This will place the image in the top-left corner of the box. The image used is shown in Figure 17.13.

Figure 17.13   Background image used to style the `<div>` element. The image should be made over 2,000 pixels long so that it will grow to the width of the widest monitors.

The <p> element must be padded on both sides to keep it away from the edges of its container. This can be achieved using `padding: 0 20px`.

The <h2> element must have the margins set to 0 so that there are no gaps at the top of the container. It must also be padded on the top right and left using `padding: 20px 20px 0 20px;`.

A background image is applied to the <h2> element using `background: url(lesson17h.jpg) no-repeat 100% 0;`. This will position the image at the right of the element. The image is shown in Figure 17.14.

FIGURE 17.14   Background image used to style the <h2> element.

Finally, the `.furtherinfo` paragraph content needs to be aligned right. This can be achieved using `text-align: right` as shown in Listing 17.9. The results can be seen in Figure 17.15.

LISTING 17.9   CSS Code for Styling the Top-Only Variation

```
div#pullquote
{
    background: #fff url(lesson17g.jpg) no-repeat;
}

div#pullquote p
{
    padding: 0 20px;
}

div#pullquote h2
{
    margin: 0;
    padding: 20px 20px 0 20px;
    background: url(lesson17h.jpg) no-repeat 100% 0;
}
```

continues

```
div#pullquote p.furtherinfo
{
    text-align: right;
}
```

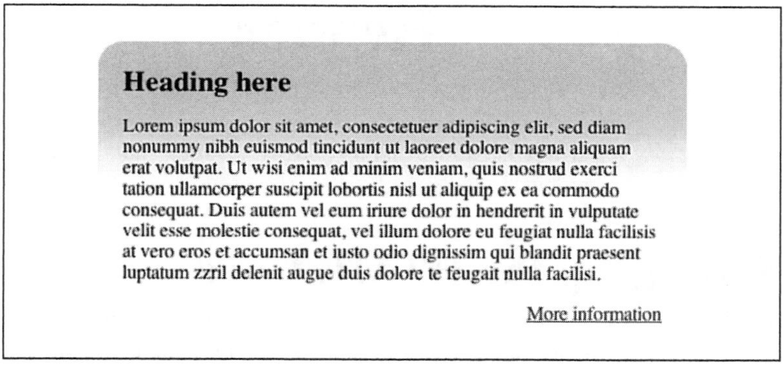

FIGURE 17.15   Screenshot of styled top-only variation.

Summary

In this lesson, you learned how to apply images to four different elements to create the illusion of a flexible, round-cornered box. You also learned how to create a fixed-width, round-cornered box and a top-only, round-cornered box. In the next lesson, you will learn how to set up and style a site header using an <h1> element, an image, and a list.

LESSON 18
Creating a Site Header

In this lesson, you will learn how to set up and style a site header using an <h1> element, an image, and a list.

Setting Up the HTML Code

The HTML code for this lesson is comprised of three main components: a <div> element, which helps define the header section semantically; an <h1> element; and a <ul> element for navigation as shown in Listing 18.1.

LISTING 18.1   HTML Code Containing the Markup for the Site Header

```
<div id="container">
    <h1>
        <a href="/"><img src="header.jpg" alt="Sitename"></a>
    </h1>
    <ul id="topnav">
        <li><a href="#">Skip to content</a></li>
        <li><a href="#">Home</a></li>
        <li><a href="#">About</a></li>
        <li><a href="#">Services</a></li>
        <li><a href="#">Staff</a></li>
        <li><a href="#">Portfolio</a></li>
        <li><a href="#">Contact</a></li>
    </ul>
</div>
```

Skip to content Link What does the `Skip to content` link mean?

This link, called a *skip link*, enables users to skip over navigation links to get to the main content of the page.

Skip links are beneficial for blind, visually impaired, and mobility impaired users, as well as people who use text browsers, mobile phones, and PDAs.

Some developers use hidden skip links, which are specifically designed for blind users. However, skip links should be visible for people who cannot use the mouse and must use tabbing to navigate websites.

Creating Selectors to Style the Header

To style the site header and its content, you will use 10 selectors as shown in Listing 18.2.

LISTING 18.2   CSS Code Showing the Selectors for Styling the Header

```
body {...}
#container {...}
h1 {...}
h1 img {...}
ul#topnav {...}
ul#topnav li {...}
ul#topnav li a:link {...}
ul#topnav li a:visited {...}
ul#topnav li a:hover {...}
ul#topnav li a:active {...}
```

Styling the <body> Element

Some browsers use margins and others use padding on the <body> element to indent content from the edges of the browser window. Because this site header sits against the top edge of the browser window, you will need to set both margins and padding to 0.

Theoretically, you should be able to apply auto margins to the left and right of a container to center it on the page. However, some browsers won't center the container using this method because they ignore the auto margins. This problem can be overcome by adding two simple declarations.

The first declaration, text-align: center, is applied to the <body> element. The second declaration, text-align: left, is added to the container rule set (see "Styling the Container" later in this lesson).

A background-color and color must also be set on the <body> element. In this case, you can use a background color of #B0BFC2 and a color of #444 as shown in Listing 18.3. The results can be seen in Figure 18.1.

LISTING 18.3   CSS Code for Styling the Body

```
body
{
    margin: 0;
    padding: 0;
    text-align: center;
    background: #B0BFC2;
    color: #444;
}
```

FIGURE 18.1   Screenshot of styled <body>.

Styling the Container

Now that the <body> element has been styled, all content will be centered on the page. This can be overcome by setting the container to text-align: left.

For browsers that support auto margins, the correct centering method is then applied: `margin: 0 auto`.

The container can be set to a width of `700px`. This width can be changed to suit your needs.

Finally, the container must be set with a white background using `background: #fff` as shown in Listing 18.4. The results can be seen in Figure 18.2.

LISTING 18.4   CSS Code for Styling the Container

```
body
{
    margin: 0;
    padding: 0;
    text-align: center;
    background: #B0BFC2;
    color: #444;
}

#container
{
    text-align: left;
    margin: 0 auto;
    width: 700px;
    background: #FFF;
}
```

FIGURE 18.2   Screenshot of styled container.

Styling the <h1> Element

As you saw in Listing 18.1, the <h1> element contains an image. This site header graphic is placed inside the <h1> element to give it greater semantic meaning. Screen readers and text-based browsers will read the alt attribute "Sitename" as if it were a text heading.

You will need to set margins and padding to 0 so that the image can sit against the top edge of the browser window.

You also can add a white border to the bottom of the <h1> element using the shorthand border: 1px solid #fff; as shown in Listing 18.5. The results can be seen in Figure 18.3.

LISTING 18.5   CSS Code for Styling the <h1> Element

```
body
{
    margin: 0;
    padding: 0;
    text-align: center;
    background: #B0BFC2;
    color: #444;
}

#container
{
    text-align: left;
    margin: 0 auto;
    width: 700px;
    background: #FFF;
}

h1
{
    margin: 0;
    padding: 0;
    border-bottom: 1px solid #fff;
}
```

Figure 18.3   Screenshot of styled <h1> element.

Styling the <image> Element

The image should be set to `display: block`. This will remove any gaps that appear below it and force the <h1> `border-bottom` to sit up against it.

The image is nested inside an <a> element. In some browsers this will cause the image to display with a 2-pixel-wide border. To avoid this, the image should be styled with `border: 0` as shown in Listing 18.6. The results can be seen in Figure 18.4.

Listing 18.6   CSS Code for Styling the <image> Element

```
body
{
    margin: 0;
    padding: 0;
    text-align: center;
    font: 85% arial, helvetica, sans-serif;
    background: #B0BFC2;
    color: #444;
}

#container
{
    text-align: left;
    margin: 0 auto;
    width: 700px;
    background: #FFF;
}

h1
```

continues

LISTING 18.6   Continued

```
{
    margin: 0;
    padding: 0;
    border-bottom: 1px solid #fff;
}

h1 img
{
    display: block;
    border: 0;
}
```

FIGURE 18.4   Screenshot of styled `<image>` element.

Styling the `<ul>` Element

As discussed in Lesson 15, "Creating Vertical Navigation," most browsers display HTML lists with left indentation. To remove this left indentation consistently across all browsers, you must override both margins and padding.

Here, you will set the margin to `0` so that the list sits up against the `<h1>` element.

The list items will need to be padded with `5px` above and below, and `10px` to the left and right. This can be achieved with a shorthand padding declaration of `padding: 5px 10px`.

The HTML bullets must be removed using `list-style-type: none`.

The `<ul>` can be styled with `background-color: #387A9B`.

Because you do not want these rules to be applied to all `<ul>` elements on the page, you should use a descendant selector that targets the topnav list only. This is achieved by using `ul#topnav` as shown in Listing 18.7. The results can be seen in Figure 18.5.

LISTING 18.7 CSS Code for Styling the `<ul>` Element

```
body
{
    margin: 0;
    padding: 0;
    text-align: center;
    font: 85% arial, helvetica, sans-serif;
    background: #B0BFC2;
    color: #444;
}

#container
{
    text-align: left;
    margin: 0 auto;
    width: 700px;
    background: #FFF;
}

h1
{
    margin: 0;
    padding: 0;
    border-bottom: 1px solid #fff;
}

h1 img
{
    display: block;
    border: 0;
}

ul#topnav
{
    margin: 0;
    padding: 5px 10px;
    list-style-type: none;
    background: #387A9B;
}
```

FIGURE 18.5   Screenshot of styled `<ul>` element.

Styling the `<li>` Element

The list must be displayed across the screen rather than down. This is achieved by setting the `<li>` to `display: inline`.

Next, a graphic bullet needs to be added to the `<li>`. The best way to do this is by using a background image set with `background: url(header-bullet.gif) no-repeat 0 50%;`. This will place one image vertically centered beside each list item.

Padding will need to be added to move the text away from the background image. In this case, `padding: 0 10px 0 8px;` will be used as shown in Listing 18.8. This will apply `10px` of padding to the right and `8px` to the left of each list item. The results can be seen in Figure 18.6.

LISTING 18.8   CSS Code for Styling the `<li>` Element

```
body
{
    margin: 0;
    padding: 0;
    text-align: center;
    font: 85% arial, helvetica, sans-serif;
    background: #B0BFC2;
    color: #444;
}

#container
{
    text-align: left;
    margin: 0 auto;
```

continues

```
        width: 700px;
        background: #FFF;
}

h1
{
        margin: 0;
        padding: 0;
        border-bottom: 1px solid #fff;
}

h1 img
{
        display: block;
        border: 0;
}

ul#topnav
{
        margin: 0;
        padding: 5px 10px;
        list-style-type: none;
        background: #387A9B;
}

ul#topnav li
{
        display: inline;
        background: url(header-bullet.gif) no-repeat 0 50%;
        padding: 0 10px 0 8px;
}
```

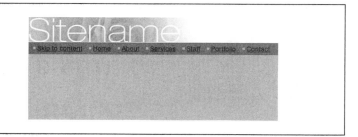

FIGURE 18.6 Screenshot of styled `<li>` element.

Styling the `<a>` Element

To avoid targeting all links on the page, a specific selector should be used. Here, you will use `ul#topnav li a:link`, `ul#topnav li a:visited`, `ul#topnav li a:hover`, and `ul#topnav li a:active`.

The link and visited pseudo-classes can be set with `text-decoration: none` (which will turn off link underlines) and `color: #FFF` as shown in Listing 18.9.

The hover and active pseudo-classes also will be set with `text-decoration: none` as well as `color: #387A9B`; and `background: #FFF`;. The results can be seen in Figure 18.7.

LISTING 18.9   CSS Code for Styling the `<a>` Element

```
body
{
    margin: 0;
    padding: 0;
    text-align: center;
    font: 85% arial, helvetica, sans-serif;
    background: #B0BFC2;
    color: #444;
}

#container
{
    text-align: left;
    margin: 0 auto;
    width: 700px;
    background: #FFF;
}

h1
{
    margin: 0;
    padding: 0;
    border-bottom: 1px solid #fff;
}

h1 img
```

continues

```
{
    display: block;
    border: 0;
}

ul#topnav
{
    margin: 0;
    padding: 5px 10px;
    list-style-type: none;
    background: #387A9B;
}

ul#topnav li
{
    display: inline;
    background: url(header-bullet.gif) no-repeat 0 50%;
    padding: 0 10px 0 8px;
}

ul#topnav li a:link, ul#topnav li a:visited
{
    text-decoration: none;
    color: #fff;
}

ul#topnav li a:hover, ul#topnav li a:active
{
    text-decoration: none;
    color: #387A9B;
    background: #fff;
}
```

FIGURE 18.7   Screenshot of styled <a> element.

Summary

In this lesson, you have learned how to center content within a browser window and style an `<h1>` element, an `<image>` element, and a `<ul>` element as links. In the next lesson, you will learn how to position a two-column page layout with a header and a footer.

LESSON 19

Positioning Two Columns with a Header and a Footer

In this lesson, you will learn how to position a two-column page layout with a header and a footer. There are many ways to position these two columns. This method involves floating them both because it is the most reliable method across most modern browsers.

Setting Up the HTML Code

The HTML code for this lesson is comprised of five main containers: an `<h1>` element, and three `<div>` elements inside an overall `<div>` container as shown in Listing 19.1.

LISTING 19.1   HTML Code Containing the Markup for a Two-Column Layout

```
<div id="container">
    <h1>
        Sitename
    </h1>
    <div id="nav">
        <ul>
            <li><a href="#">Home</a></li>
            <li><a href="#">About us</a></li>
            <li><a href="#">Services</a></li>
            <li><a href="#">Staff</a></li>
            <li><a href="#">Portfolio</a></li>
            <li><a href="#">Contact us</a></li>
        </ul>
```

continues

LISTING 19.1   Continued

```
    </div>
    <div id="content">
        <h2>
            About Sitename
        </h2>
        <p>
            Lorem ipsum dolor....
        </p>
        <p>
            Ut wisi enim ad...
        </p>
    </div>
    <div id="footer">
        Copyright &copy; Sitename 2005
    </div>
</div>
```

Creating Selectors to Style the Two-Column Layout

To style the two-column layout and its content, you will use 12 selectors as shown in Listing 19.2.

LISTING 19.2   CSS Code Showing the Selectors for Styling a Two-Column Layout

```
body {...}
#container {...}
h1 {...}
#nav {...}
#nav ul {...}
#nav li {...}
#content {...}
#footer {...}
h2 {...}
a:link {...}
a:visited {...}
a:hover, a:active {...}
```

Styling the <body> Element

As discussed in Lesson 18, "Creating a Site Header," to center a container on the page, you must find ways to work around browsers that don't support auto margins. The first work-around involves applying text-align: center to the <body> element as shown in Listing 19.3. The results can be seen in Figure 19.1.

A background-color and color also must be set on the <body> element. You can use a background color of #B0BFC2 and a color of #444.

LISTING 19.3   CSS Code for Styling the Body

```
body
{
    text-align: center;
    background: #B0BFC2;
    color: #444;
}
```

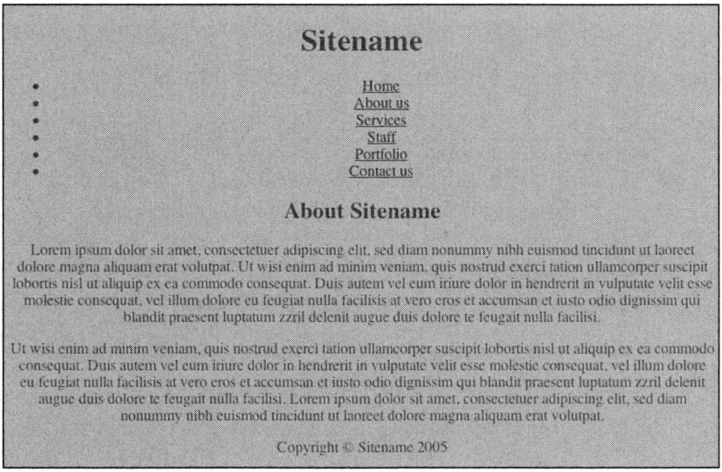

FIGURE 19.1   Screenshot of styled <body>.

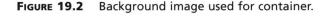

Styling the Container

Now that the <body> element has been styled, all content will be centered on the page. This can be overcome by setting the container to text-align: left.

For browsers that support auto margins, the correct centering method is then applied: margin: 0 auto.

The container can be set to a width of 700px. This width can be changed to suit your needs.

Finally, the container must be set with a background image using background: #FFF url(header-base.gif) repeat-y; as shown in Listing 19.4.

The background image can be seen in Figure 19.2 and the results are shown in Figure 19.3.

Figure 19.2   Background image used for container.

>
>
> **Creating the Illusion of Column Colors**   One problem with floating containers is that they will generally only extend to the depth of their content. If one column is much shorter than another, it can be very hard to create columns using background colors alone.
>
> So, how do you get the shorter column's background color to extend to the bottom of the page?
>
> One simple solution is to use a background image that gives the illusion of column colors. This image can be added to the overall container as a background image and repeated down the y axis.
>
> The floated containers then sit over the top of this repeated image, and the colors will extend to the bottom of the page, no matter which column is longer.

LISTING 19.4   CSS Code for Styling the Container

```
body
{
    text-align: center;
    background: #B0BFC2;
    color: #444;
}

#container
{
    text-align: left;
    margin: 0 auto;
    width: 700px;
    background: #FFF url(header-base.gif) repeat-y;
}
```

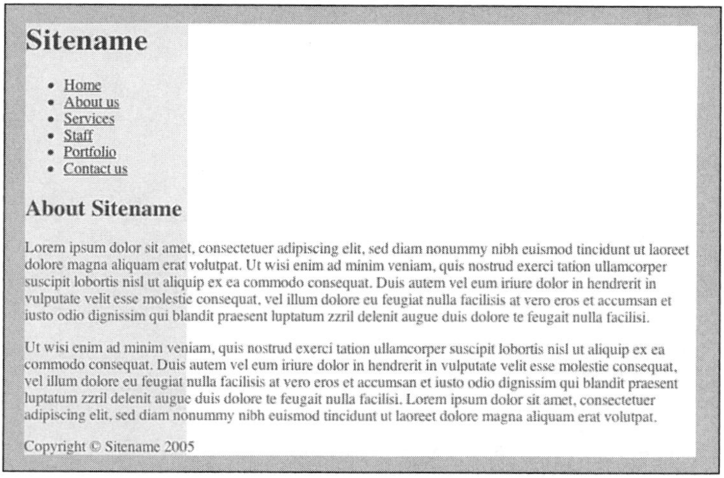

FIGURE 19.3   Screenshot of styled container.

Styling the <h1> Element

The first step in styling the heading is to set a background color. You can use background: #D36832. The color can then be set to #fff.

Next, padding: 20px can be applied to create some space around the
<h1> content.

You will then need to set margin: 0 to remove the default top and bottom
margins.

You also can add a border to the bottom of the <h1> element using the
shorthand border: 5px solid #387A9B; as shown in Listing 19.5. The
results can be seen in Figure 19.4.

LISTING 19.5   CSS Code for Styling the <h1> Element

```
body
{
    text-align: center;
    background: #B0BFC2;
    color: #444;
}

#container
{
    text-align: left;
    margin: 0 auto;
    width: 700px;
    background: #FFF url(header-base.gif) repeat-y;
}

h1
{
    background: #D36832;
    color: #FFF;
    padding: 20px;
    margin: 0;
    border-bottom: 5px solid #387A9B;
}
```

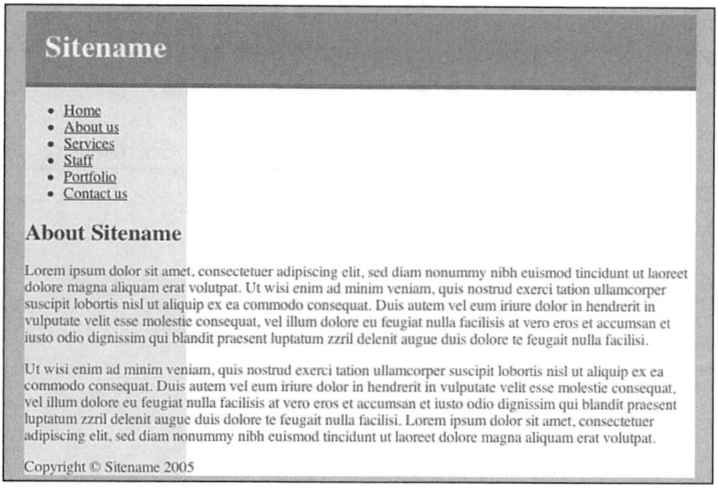

FIGURE 19.4   Screenshot of styled <h1> element.

Styling the #nav Container

To position the #nav container and #content container beside each other, they will both need to be floated.

To float the #nav container, use float: left. You also will need to set a width, which in this case will be 130px.

Internet Explorer 5 and 5.5 for Windows will sometimes display margins at double the specified width in certain circumstances. This *Double Margin Float Bug* is explained in Lesson 11, "Positioning an Image and Its Caption." The bug can be fixed by setting the floated item to display: inline. All other browsers will ignore this declaration, but Internet Explorer 5 and 5.5 for Windows will then apply the correct margin width.

Now that the margins will display correctly in all recent browsers, you can apply margin-left: 20px.

Finally, padding needs to be applied to the top and bottom of the container. Here, you will need to use padding: 15px 0 as shown in Listing 19.6. The results can be seen in Figure 19.5.

LISTING 19.6   CSS Code for Styling the #nav Container

```
body
{
    text-align: center;
    background: #B0BFC2;
    color: #444;
}

#container
{
    text-align: left;
    margin: 0 auto;
    width: 700px;
    background: #FFF url(header-base.gif) repeat-y;
}

h1
{
    background: #D36832;
    color: #FFF;
    padding: 20px;
    margin: 0;
    border-bottom: 5px solid #387A9B;
}

#nav
{
    float: left;
    width: 130px;
    display: inline;
    margin-left: 20px;
    padding: 15px 0;
}
```

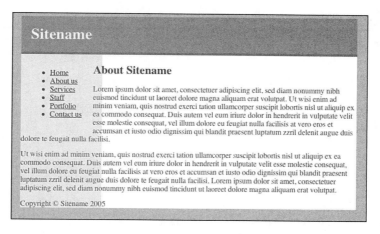

Figure 19.5   Screenshot of styled #nav container.

Styling the `<ul>` Element

Both the margins and padding of the `<ul>` need to be set to 0 to remove any browser default styling.

To remove list bullets, use `list-style-type: none`.

The list items will need to be aligned against the right edge of the #nav container. This can be achieved using `text-align: right` as shown in Listing 19.7. The results can be seen in Figure 19.6.

LISTING 19.7   CSS Code for Styling the `<ul>` Element

```
body
{
    text-align: center;
    background: #B0BFC2;
    color: #444;
}
```

continues

LISTING 19.7   Continued

```
#container
{
    text-align: left;
    margin: 0 auto;
    width: 700px;
    background: #FFF url(header-base.gif) repeat-y;
}

h1
{
    background: #D36832;
    color: #FFF;
    padding: 20px;
    margin: 0;
    border-bottom: 5px solid #387A9B;
}

#nav
{
    float: left;
    width: 130px;
    display: inline;
    margin-left: 20px;
    padding: 15px 0;
}

#nav ul
{
    margin: 0;
    padding: 0;
    list-style-type: none;
    text-align: right;
}
```

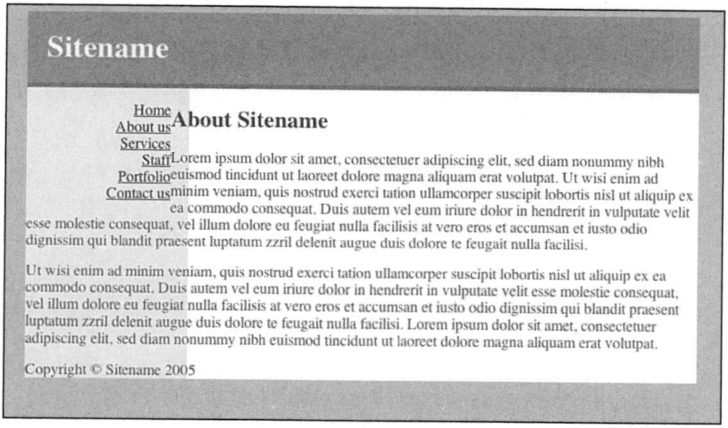

FIGURE 19.6   Screenshot of styled `<ul>` element.

Styling the `<li>` Element

The list items will now have a background image applied to them to act as a bullet. You will use `background: url(header-bullet.gif) no-repeat 100% .4em;` to place the background image against the right edge of the `<li>` element, and .4em from the top. The image is also set to `no-repeat`, so it does not repeat across the entire `<li>` element.

Padding can then be applied to the right edge and bottom of the `<li>`. The right padding will move the list content away from the edge so that it does not appear over the top of the background image. The bottom padding is used to provide some space between list items as shown in Listing 19.8. The results can be seen in Figure 19.7.

LISTING 19.8   CSS Code for Styling the `<li>` Element

```
body
{
    text-align: center;
    background: #B0BFC2;
    color: #444;
}
```

continues

LISTING 19.8   Continued

```
#container
{
    text-align: left;
    margin: 0 auto;
    width: 700px;
    background: #FFF url(header-base.gif) repeat-y;
}

h1
{
    background: #D36832;
    color: #FFF;
    padding: 20px;
    margin: 0;
    border-bottom: 5px solid #387A9B;
}

#nav
{
    float: left;
    width: 130px;
    display: inline;
    margin-left: 20px;
    padding: 15px 0;
}

#nav ul
{
    margin: 0;
    padding: 0;
    list-style-type: none;
    text-align: right;
}

#nav li
{
    background: url(header-bullet.gif) no-repeat 100% .4em;
    padding: 0 10px 5px 0;
}
```

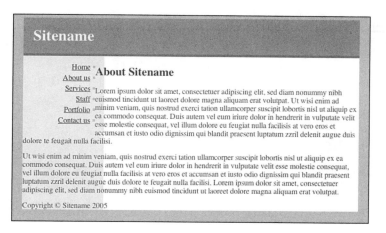

FIGURE 19.7   Screenshot of styled `<li>` element.

Styling the #content Container

The #content container needs to be set to `float: left` so that it sits beside the #nav container. You also will need to set a width, which in this case will be `475px`.

To create a gutter between the two columns, use `margin-left: 45px`.

Finally, padding needs to be applied to the top and bottom of the container. You will need to use `padding: 15px 0` as shown in Listing 19.9. The results can be seen in Figure 19.8.

LISTING 19.9   CSS Code for Styling the #content Container

```css
body
{
    text-align: center;
    background: #B0BFC2;
    color: #444;
}

#container
{
    text-align: left;
```

continues

LISTING 19.9   Continued

```
    margin: 0 auto;
    width: 700px;
    background: #FFF url(header-base.gif) repeat-y;
}

h1
{
    background: #D36832;
    color: #FFF;
    padding: 20px;
    margin: 0;
    border-bottom: 5px solid #387A9B;
}

#nav
{
    float: left;
    width: 130px;
    display: inline;
    margin-left: 20px;
    padding: 15px 0;
}

#nav ul
{
    margin: 0;
    padding: 0;
    list-style-type: none;
    text-align: right;
}

#nav li
{
    background: url(header-bullet.gif) no-repeat 100% .4em;
    padding: 0 10px 5px 0;
}

#content
{
    float: left;
    width: 475px;
    margin-left: 45px;
    padding: 15px 0;
}
```

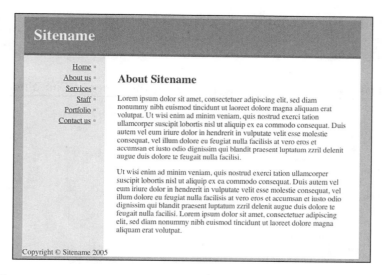

FIGURE 19.8   Screenshot of styled #content container.

Styling the #footer Container

The #footer container is displayed after the #nav and #content containers. Because these two containers are floated, there is a possibility that the #footer container might try to sit beside them. This can be fixed using the clear property on the #footer container. The four options are clear: left, clear: right, clear: both, and clear: none.

Here you will use clear: both, which will force the #footer container to sit below the two floated containers.

To set a background color, use background: #387A9B. The color can then be set to #fff.

Next, padding can be used to create some space around the content. You can apply 5px to the top and bottom, and 10px to the left and right edges using padding: 5px 10px as shown in Listing 19.10.

To align the footer content to the right, use text-align: right.

Finally, the font size of the footer can be reduced because it is less important information. You can use font-size: 80% as shown in Listing 19.10. The results can be seen in Figure 19.9.

LISTING 19.10   CSS Code for Styling the `#footer` Container

```
body
{
    text-align: center;
    background: #B0BFC2;
    color: #444;
}

#container
{
    text-align: left;
    margin: 0 auto;
    width: 700px;
    background: #FFF url(header-base.gif) repeat-y;
}

h1
{
    background: #D36832;
    color: #FFF;
    padding: 20px;
    margin: 0;
    border-bottom: 5px solid #387A9B;
}

#nav
{
    float: left;
    width: 130px;
    display: inline;
    margin-left: 20px;
    padding: 15px 0;
}

#nav ul
{
    margin: 0;
    padding: 0;
    list-style-type: none;
    text-align: right;
}
```

continues

```
#nav li
{
    background: url(header-bullet.gif) no-repeat 100% .4em;
    padding: 0 10px 5px 0;
}

#content
{
    float: left;
    width: 475px;
    margin-left: 45px;
    padding: 15px 0;
}

#footer
{
    clear: both;
    background: #387A9B;
    color: #fff;
    padding: 5px 10px;
    text-align: right;
    font-size: 80%;
}
```

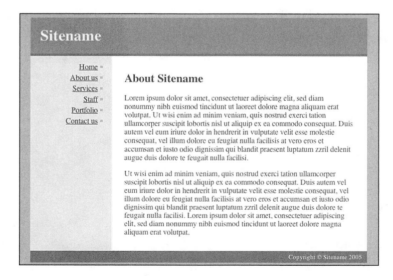

FIGURE 19.9   Screenshot of styled #footer container.

Styling the <h2> Element

The <h2> element is used for the main heading on the page. Its top margin needs to be removed so that the <h2> element lines up with the content in the #nav container. This is achieved using margin-top: 0.

Next, the color can be changed using color: #B23B00.

Standard headings generally are displayed in bold text. You can override this default behavior using font-weight: normal as shown in Listing 19.11. The results can be seen in Figure 19.10.

LISTING 19.11   CSS Code for Styling the <h2> Element

```
body
{
    text-align: center;
    background: #B0BFC2;
    color: #444;
}

#container
{
    text-align: left;
    margin: 0 auto;
    width: 700px;
    background: #FFF url(header-base.gif) repeat-y;
}

h1
{
    background: #D36832;
    color: #FFF;
    padding: 20px;
    margin: 0;
    border-bottom: 5px solid #387A9B;
}

#nav
{
    float: left;
    width: 130px;
```

continues

```
        display: inline;
        margin-left: 20px;
        padding: 15px 0;
}

#nav ul
{
        margin: 0;
        padding: 0;
        list-style-type: none;
        text-align: right;
}

#nav li
{
        background: url(header-bullet.gif) no-repeat 100% .4em;
        padding: 0 10px 5px 0;
}

#content
{
        float: left;
        width: 475px;
        margin-left: 45px;
        padding: 15px 0;
}

#footer
{
        clear: both;
        background: #387A9B;
        color: #fff;
        padding: 5px 10px;
        text-align: right;
        font-size: 80%;
}

h2
{
        margin-top: 0;
        color: #B23B00;
        font-weight: normal;
}
```

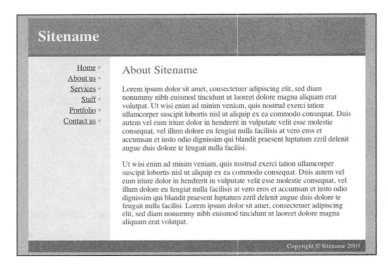

FIGURE 19.10   Screenshot of styled <h2> element.

Styling the <a> Element

The final step in this lesson involves setting the link colors. You will work on four pseudo-classes.

The a:link pseudo-class can be set to color: #175B7D, and the a:visited pseudo-class can be set to color: #600.

The a:hover and a:active pseudo-classes also can be set with color: #fff; and background: #175B7D as shown in Listing 19.12. The results can be seen in Figure 19.11.

LISTING 19.12   CSS Code for Styling the <h2> Element

```
body
{
    text-align: center;
    background: #B0BFC2;
    color: #444;
}

#container
```

continues

```
{
    text-align: left;
    margin: 0 auto;
    width: 700px;
    background: #FFF url(header-base.gif) repeat-y;
}

h1
{
    background: #D36832;
    color: #FFF;
    padding: 20px;
    margin: 0;
    border-bottom: 5px solid #387A9B;
}

#nav
{
    float: left;
    width: 130px;
    display: inline;
    margin-left: 20px;
    padding: 15px 0;
}

#nav ul
{
    margin: 0;
    padding: 0;
    list-style-type: none;
    text-align: right;
}

#nav li
{
    background: url(header-bullet.gif) no-repeat 100% .4em;
    padding: 0 10px 5px 0;
}

#content
{
    float: left;
    width: 475px;
    margin-left: 45px;
```

continues

LISTING 19.12   Continued

```
    padding: 15px 0;
}

#footer
{
    clear: both;
    background: #387A9B;
    color: #fff;
    padding: 5px 10px;
    text-align: right;
    font-size: 80%;
}

h2
{
    margin-top: 0;
    color: #B23B00;
    font-weight: normal;
}

a:link
{
    color: #175B7D;
}

a:visited
{
    color: #600;
}

a:hover, a:active
{
    color: #fff;
    background: #175B7D;
}
```

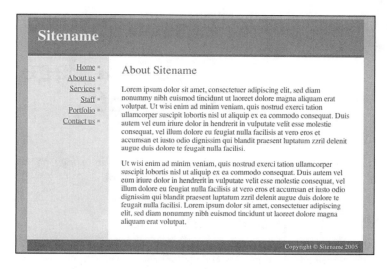

FIGURE 19.11   Screenshot of styled <a> element.

Summary

In this lesson, you learned how to center content within a browser window, style an <h1> element, and position and style two columns and a footer. In the next lesson, you will learn how to style a page for print using CSS.

LESSON 20
Styling a Page for Print

In this lesson, you will learn how to style a page for print using CSS. You will also learn about the media type and how it is used.

Setting Up the Print CSS

In the past, many sites provided two versions of each page—one designed for the screen and the other designed to be printed. The two versions generally used the same content, but were presented in different ways.

One advantage of CSS is that you can style a page for print without the need for additional pages. This is achieved using the media attribute, which can be applied to external style sheet links (as shown in Listing 20.1) or to the style element for embedded styles (as shown in Listing 20.2).

LISTING 20.1   HTML Code Containing a Link to an External Style Sheet with a Media Value of screen

```
<link rel="stylesheet" href="lesson20.css" type="text/css"
media="screen">
```

LISTING 20.2   HTML Code Containing an Embedded Style Sheet with a Media Value of screen

```
<style type="text/css" media="screen">
<!--
... Screen style rules go here ...
-->
</style>
```

If your layout needs to be identical for screen and print, the media attribute value can be set to all as shown in Listing 20.3 (for external style sheets) and Listing 20.4 (for embedded styles).

LISTING 20.3 HTML Code Containing a Link to an External Style Sheet with a Media Value of all

```
<link rel="stylesheet" href="lesson20.css" type="text/css"
media="all">
```

LISTING 20.4 HTML Code Containing an Embedded Style Sheet with a Media Value of all

```
<style type="text/css" media="all">
<!--
... All style rules go here ...
-->
</style>
```

If the layout needs to be different for screen and print, the media attribute values can be set to screen and print as shown in Listings 20.5 and 20.6.

LISTING 20.5 HTML Code Containing Links to External Style Sheets with Media Values Set to screen and print

```
<link rel="stylesheet" href="lesson20.css" type="text/css"
media="screen">
<link rel="stylesheet" href="lesson20-print.css"
type="text/css" media="print">
```

LISTING 20.6 HTML Code Containing Embedded Style Sheets with Media Values Set to screen and print

```
<style type="text/css" media="screen">
<!--
... Screen style rules go here ...
-->
</style>

<style type="text/css" media="print">
<!--
... Print style rules go here ...
-->
</style>
```

Media Types and Older Browsers   There are currently 10 media types within the CSS2 Specification. They are

- `all`—Suitable for all devices

- `aural`—For speech synthesizers

- `braille`—For Braille tactile-feedback devices

- `embossed`—For paged Braille printers

- `handheld`—For handheld devices such as mobile phones and PDAs

- `print`—For print material and for documents viewed in Print Preview mode

- `projection`—For projected presentations

- `screen`—For color computer screens

- `tty`—For media using fixed-pitch character grids such as teletypes and terminals

- `tv`—For television-type devices

Multiple media types can be provided within the same attribute as long as they are separated by commas. For example, you could use `media="print, projection"` to target these media types only.

If no media type is specified, `screen` will be applied because it is the default value.

Some early browsers, such as Netscape Navigator 4, do not understand the `all` media type or comma-separated media types. If you intend to support these browsers, it might be best to specify `screen` or no media type at all.

Starting with Existing HTML and CSS Code

For this lesson, you will use the HTML code from Lesson 19, "Positioning Two Columns with a Header and a Footer," as shown in Listing 20.7 and rework it for print.

LISTING 20.7   HTML Code Containing the Markup for a Two-Column Layout

```
<div id="container">
    <h1>
        Sitename
    </h1>
    <div id="nav">
        <ul>
            <li><a href="#">Home</a></li>
            <li><a href="#">About us</a></li>
            <li><a href="#">Services</a></li>
            <li><a href="#">Staff</a></li>
            <li><a href="#">Portfolio</a></li>
            <li><a href="#">Contact us</a></li>
        </ul>
    </div>
    <div id="content">
        <h2>
            About Sitename
        </h2>
        <p>
            Lorem ipsum dolor....
        </p>
        <p>
            Ut wisi enim ad...
        </p>
    </div>
    <div id="footer">
        Copyright &copy; Sitename 2005
    </div>
</div>
```

Creating Selectors to Style for Print

To style the two-column layout for print, you will use five selectors as shown in Listing 20.8.

LISTING 20.8   CSS Code Showing the Selectors for Styling the Two-Column Layout for Print

```
body {...}
h1 {...}
#nav {...}
#footer {...}
a {...}
```

 Some Warnings About Styling for Print   When styling pages for print, you should be aware that floated containers and complex absolute positioning can cause problems in some browsers.

Long floated containers can cause problems in some versions of Mozilla and Netscape. These browsers sometimes have trouble calculating the length of floated containers and will only print the first page of the container's content.

Complex absolute positioning (also layouts that need to be pixel perfect) can cause problems for Internet Explorer 6. This browser has been known to crash when using Print Preview to view absolutely positioned layouts.

Although some floated and absolutely positioned content can be used, it is best to keep the overall layout as simple as possible when styling for print.

Many browsers do not print *background images* as a default. For this reason, background images should not be used to display information that is critical to the reader.

Styling the <body> Element

The <body> element will be styled with font, color, and background declarations as shown in Listing 20.9.

The font property will be used to determine the base font size and family for all elements on the page. In this example, 100% has been used because it enables the user to control the font size. A serif font has been chosen because it is more readable in print, whereas a sans-serif font is more readable on a screen or monitor (small cell phone screens in particular make serif type difficult to read). These can be changed to suit your needs.

No margins or padding have been specified for the <body> element; these will be determined by the printer. The results can be seen in Figure 20.1.

LISTING 20.9   CSS Code for Styling the Body

```
body
{
    font: 100% georgia, times, serif;
    background: #fff;
    color: #000;
}
```

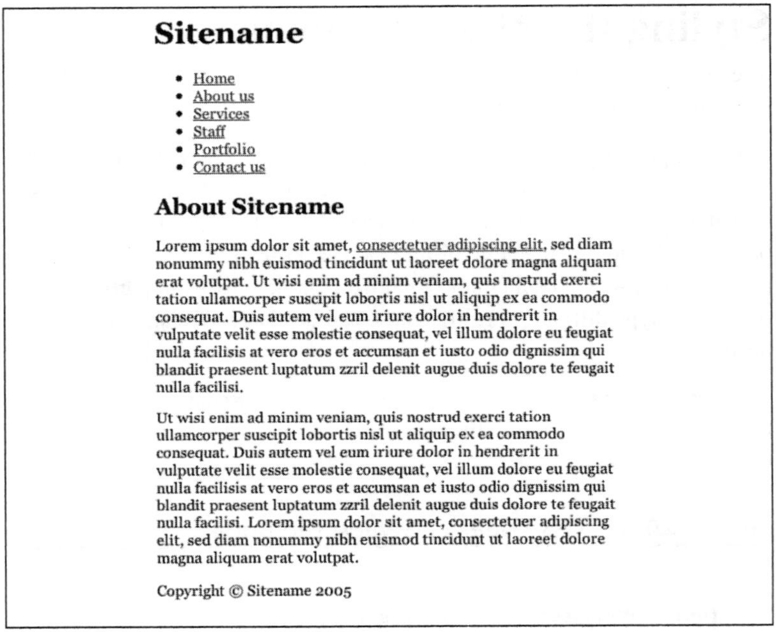

Sitename

- Home
- About us
- Services
- Staff
- Portfolio
- Contact us

About Sitename

Lorem ipsum dolor sit amet, consectetuer adipiscing elit, sed diam nonummy nibh euismod tincidunt ut laoreet dolore magna aliquam erat volutpat. Ut wisi enim ad minim veniam, quis nostrud exerci tation ullamcorper suscipit lobortis nisl ut aliquip ex ea commodo consequat. Duis autem vel eum iriure dolor in hendrerit in vulputate velit esse molestie consequat, vel illum dolore eu feugiat nulla facilisis at vero eros et accumsan et iusto odio dignissim qui blandit praesent luptatum zzril delenit augue duis dolore te feugait nulla facilisi.

Ut wisi enim ad minim veniam, quis nostrud exerci tation ullamcorper suscipit lobortis nisl ut aliquip ex ea commodo consequat. Duis autem vel eum iriure dolor in hendrerit in vulputate velit esse molestie consequat, vel illum dolore eu feugiat nulla facilisis at vero eros et accumsan et iusto odio dignissim qui blandit praesent luptatum zzril delenit augue duis dolore te feugait nulla facilisi. Lorem ipsum dolor sit amet, consectetuer adipiscing elit, sed diam nonummy nibh euismod tincidunt ut laoreet dolore magna aliquam erat volutpat.

Copyright © Sitename 2005

FIGURE 20.1   Screenshot of styled <body>.

Styling the <h1> Element

The <h1> element will be styled very simply with `border-bottom` and `margin-bottom` as shown in Listing 20.10 and Figure 20.2.

Listing 20.10   CSS Code for Styling the <h1> Element

```
body
{
    font: 100% georgia, times, serif;
    background: #fff;
    color: #000;
}

h1
{

    border-bottom: 1px solid #999;
    margin-bottom: 1em;
}
```

What Is an Em? In traditional typesetting, an *em space* is defined as the width of an uppercase *M* in the current face and point size. An *em dash* is the width of a capital *M*, an *en dash* is half the width of a capital *M*, and an *em quad* (a unit of spacing material typically used for paragraph indentation) is the square of a capital *M*.

In CSS, an em is a relative measure of length that inherits size information from parent elements. If the parent element is the <body>, the size of the element is actually determined by the user's browser font settings. So in most browsers, where the default font size is 16px, 1em will be 16px.

Sitename

- Home
- About us
- Services
- Staff
- Portfolio
- Contact us

About Sitename

Lorem ipsum dolor sit amet, consectetuer adipiscing elit, sed diam nonummy nibh euismod tincidunt ut laoreet dolore magna aliquam erat volutpat. Ut wisi enim ad minim veniam, quis nostrud exerci tation ullamcorper suscipit lobortis nisl ut aliquip ex ea commodo consequat. Duis autem vel eum iriure dolor in hendrerit in vulputate velit esse molestie consequat, vel illum dolore eu feugiat nulla facilisis at vero eros et accumsan et iusto odio dignissim qui blandit praesent luptatum zzril delenit augue duis dolore te feugait nulla facilisi.

Ut wisi enim ad minim veniam, quis nostrud exerci tation ullamcorper suscipit lobortis nisl ut aliquip ex ea commodo consequat. Duis autem vel eum iriure dolor in hendrerit in vulputate velit esse molestie consequat, vel illum dolore eu feugiat nulla facilisis at vero eros et accumsan et iusto odio dignissim qui blandit praesent luptatum zzril delenit augue duis dolore te feugait nulla facilisi. Lorem ipsum dolor sit amet, consectetuer adipiscing elit, sed diam nonummy nibh euismod tincidunt ut laoreet dolore magna aliquam erat volutpat.

Copyright © Sitename 2005

FIGURE 20.2   Screenshot of styled <h1>.

Hiding Content from the Printer   Some website content has no purpose on a printed page, such as site-based navigation or some advertising.

These areas of content can be hidden from the printer using `display: none;`.

When this declaration is applied to an element, the elements and all descendants will not be displayed. You cannot override this behavior by setting a different display property on the descendant elements.

Styling the #nav Container

To remove the navigation from the printed page, use `display: none;` as shown in Listing 20.11. The results can be seen in Figure 20.3.

LISTING 20.11   CSS Code for Styling the #nav Container

```
body
{
    font: 100% georgia, times, serif;
    background: #fff;
    color: #000;
}

h1
{
    border-bottom: 1px solid #999;
    margin-bottom: 1em;
}

#nav
{
    display: none;
}
```

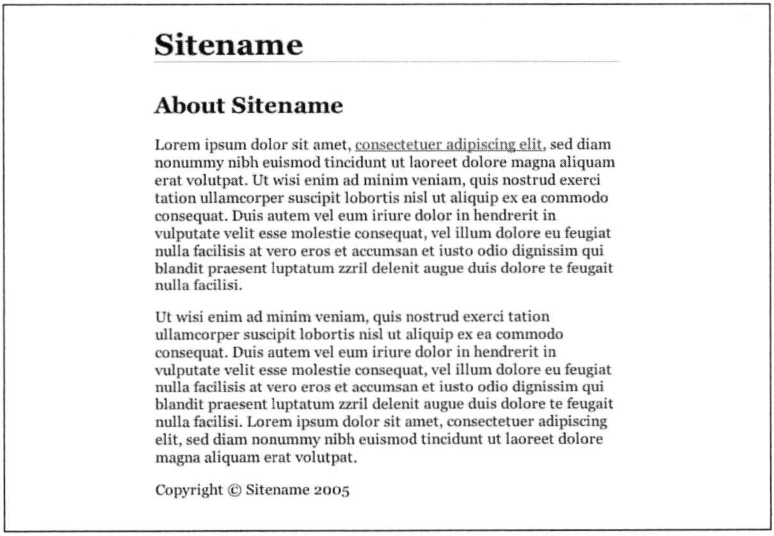

Sitename

About Sitename

Lorem ipsum dolor sit amet, consectetuer adipiscing elit, sed diam nonummy nibh euismod tincidunt ut laoreet dolore magna aliquam erat volutpat. Ut wisi enim ad minim veniam, quis nostrud exerci tation ullamcorper suscipit lobortis nisl ut aliquip ex ea commodo consequat. Duis autem vel eum iriure dolor in hendrerit in vulputate velit esse molestie consequat, vel illum dolore eu feugiat nulla facilisis at vero eros et accumsan et iusto odio dignissim qui blandit praesent luptatum zzril delenit augue duis dolore te feugait nulla facilisi.

Ut wisi enim ad minim veniam, quis nostrud exerci tation ullamcorper suscipit lobortis nisl ut aliquip ex ea commodo consequat. Duis autem vel eum iriure dolor in hendrerit in vulputate velit esse molestie consequat, vel illum dolore eu feugiat nulla facilisis at vero eros et accumsan et iusto odio dignissim qui blandit praesent luptatum zzril delenit augue duis dolore te feugait nulla facilisi. Lorem ipsum dolor sit amet, consectetuer adipiscing elit, sed diam nonummy nibh euismod tincidunt ut laoreet dolore magna aliquam erat volutpat.

Copyright © Sitename 2005

FIGURE 20.3   Screenshot of styled #nav container.

Styling the `#footer` Container

The footer can be separated from other content using `border-top` and `margin-top` properties.

The footer content also can be right-aligned using the `text-align` property.

To add space between the border and footer content, `padding-top` can be used as shown in Listing 20.12. The results can be seen in Figure 20.4.

LISTING 20.12   CSS Code for Styling the `#footer` Container

```
body
{
    font: 100% georgia, times, serif;
    background: #fff;
    color: #000;
}

h1
```

continues

LISTING 20.12   Continued

```
{
    border-bottom: 1px solid #999;
    margin-bottom: 1em;
}

#nav
{
    display: none;
}

#footer
{
    border-top: 1px solid #999;
    text-align: right;
    margin-top: 3em;
    padding-top: 1em;
}
```

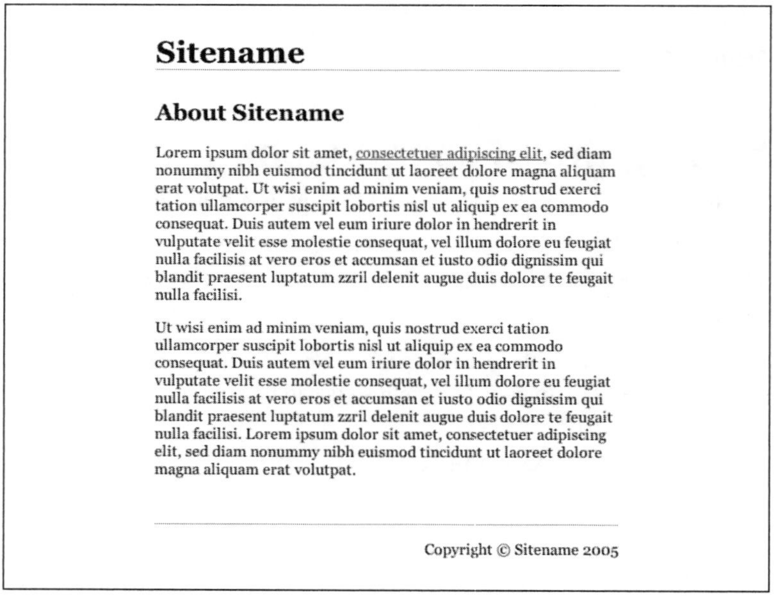

Sitename

About Sitename

Lorem ipsum dolor sit amet, consectetuer adipiscing elit, sed diam
nonummy nibh euismod tincidunt ut laoreet dolore magna aliquam
erat volutpat. Ut wisi enim ad minim veniam, quis nostrud exerci
tation ullamcorper suscipit lobortis nisl ut aliquip ex ea commodo
consequat. Duis autem vel eum iriure dolor in hendrerit in
vulputate velit esse molestie consequat, vel illum dolore eu feugiat
nulla facilisis at vero eros et accumsan et iusto odio dignissim qui
blandit praesent luptatum zzril delenit augue duis dolore te feugait
nulla facilisi.

Ut wisi enim ad minim veniam, quis nostrud exerci tation
ullamcorper suscipit lobortis nisl ut aliquip ex ea commodo
consequat. Duis autem vel eum iriure dolor in hendrerit in
vulputate velit esse molestie consequat, vel illum dolore eu feugiat
nulla facilisi at vero eros et accumsan et iusto odio dignissim qui
blandit praesent luptatum zzril delenit augue duis dolore te feugait
nulla facilisi. Lorem ipsum dolor sit amet, consectetuer adipiscing
elit, sed diam nonummy nibh euismod tincidunt ut laoreet dolore
magna aliquam erat volutpat.

Copyright © Sitename 2005

FIGURE 20.4   Screenshot of styled #footer container.

Styling the <a> Element

Hyperlinks have no real value on a printed page. To make links appear the same as all other content, you could set the color to *#000* and then turn off underlines with text-decoration: none; as shown in Listing 20.13. The final result can be seen in Figure 20.5.

LISTING 20.13   CSS Code for Styling the <a> Element

```
body
{
    font: 100% georgia, times, serif;
    background: #fff;
    color: #000;
}

h1
{
    border-bottom: 1px solid #999;
    margin-bottom: 1em;
}

#nav
{
    display: none;
}

#footer
{
    border-top: 1px solid #999;
    text-align: right;
    margin-top: 3em;
    padding-top: 1em;
}

a
{
    color: #000;
    text-decoration: none;
}
```

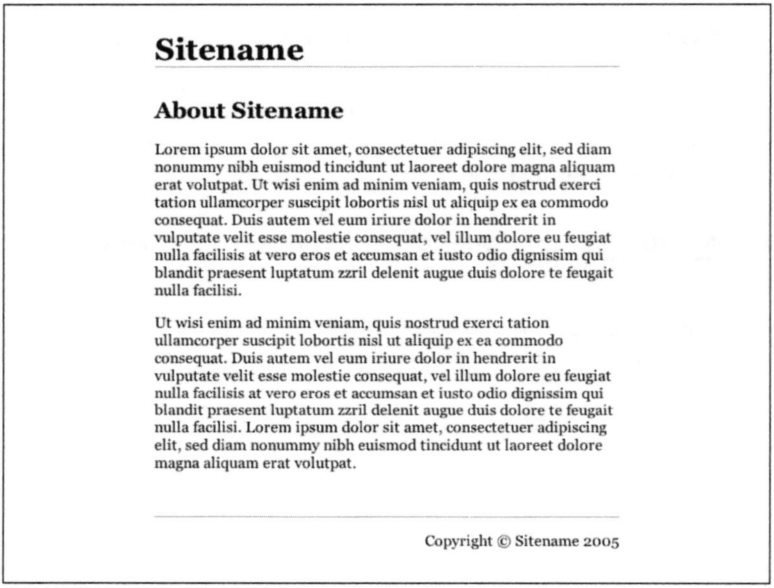

Sitename

About Sitename

Lorem ipsum dolor sit amet, consectetuer adipiscing elit, sed diam
nonummy nibh euismod tincidunt ut laoreet dolore magna aliquam
erat volutpat. Ut wisi enim ad minim veniam, quis nostrud exerci
tation ullamcorper suscipit lobortis nisl ut aliquip ex ea commodo
consequat. Duis autem vel eum iriure dolor in hendrerit in
vulputate velit esse molestie consequat, vel illum dolore eu feugiat
nulla facilisis at vero eros et accumsan et iusto odio dignissim qui
blandit praesent luptatum zzril delenit augue duis dolore te feugait
nulla facilisi.

Ut wisi enim ad minim veniam, quis nostrud exerci tation
ullamcorper suscipit lobortis nisl ut aliquip ex ea commodo
consequat. Duis autem vel eum iriure dolor in hendrerit in
vulputate velit esse molestie consequat, vel illum dolore eu feugiat
nulla facilisis at vero eros et accumsan et iusto odio dignissim qui
blandit praesent luptatum zzril delenit augue duis dolore te feugait
nulla facilisi. Lorem ipsum dolor sit amet, consectetuer adipiscing
elit, sed diam nonummy nibh euismod tincidunt ut laoreet dolore
magna aliquam erat volutpat.

Copyright © Sitename 2005

FIGURE 20.5   Screenshot of styled <a> element.

Summary

In this lesson, you have learned how to style a layout specifically for print
using the media attribute. In the next lesson, you will learn how to position a three-column liquid layout with a header and a footer.

LESSON 21

Positioning Three Columns with a Header and a Footer

In this lesson, you will learn how to position a three-column liquid layout with a header and a footer. This method involves placing background images inside two containers to give the illusion of column colors, and then floating all three columns.

Setting Up the HTML Code

Although tables can be used to create HTML page layouts, they are not ideal. Pages laid out with tables are often much larger in size due to the additional markup that is required. They are also less flexible, so it is harder to move sections of the layout without restructuring the markup completely.

CSS-based layouts, on the other hand, are generally smaller in file size and much more flexible.

The HTML code for this lesson is comprised of seven main containers—an `<h1>` element and six `<div>` elements as shown in Listing 21.1.

LISTING 21.1   HTML Code Containing the Markup for a Three-Column Layout

```
<h1>
    Sitename
</h1>
<div id="container">
```

continues

LISTING 21.1   Continued

```
<div id="container2">
    <div id="content">
        <h2>
            Page heading
        </h2>
        <p>
            Lorem ipsum dolor sit amet...
        </p>
    </div>
    <div id="news">
        <h3>
            News
        </h3>
        <p>
            Lorem ipsum dolor sit amet...
        </p>
    </div>
    <div id="nav">
        <h3>
            Sections
        </h3>
        <ul>
            <li><a href="#">Home</a></li>
            <li><a href="#">About us</a></li>
            <li><a href="#">Services</a></li>
            <li><a href="#">Staff</a></li>
            <li><a href="#">Portfolio</a></li>
            <li><a href="#">Contact us</a></li>
        </ul>
    </div>
    <div id="footer">
        Copyright &copy; Sitename 2005
    </div>
</div>
</div>
```

Creating Selectors to Style the Three-Column Layout

To style the three-column layout and its content, you will use 10 selectors as shown in Listing 21.2.

LISTING 21.2   CSS Code Showing the Selectors for Styling the Three-Column Layout

```
body {...}
h1 {...}
h2, h3, p {...}
#container {...}
#container2 {...}
#content {...}
#news {...}
#nav {...}
#nav ul {...}
#footer {...}
```

What Is a Liquid Layout?   There are four main methods used to lay out web pages. They are

- **Liquid layout**—All containers on the page have their widths defined in percents. A liquid layout will resize when you resize your browser window.

- **Combination liquid and fixed layout**—Similar to liquid layouts, except one or more of the containers on the page have fixed widths.

- **Fixed-width layout**—All containers on the page have their widths defined in pixels or other fixed units. A fixed layout will not move in and out when you resize your browser window.

- **Em-driven layout**—All containers on the page have their widths defined in ems. The containers will scale according to the user's current browser font size. These layouts will not move when the browser window is resized.

You also can use combinations of the preceding list.

Creating a Liquid-Layout Grid

When creating a liquid layout, it is important to include vertical gutters so that the content columns do not butt up against each other. All widths should be set in percentages so that the entire page can be resized as a single unit, depending on the size of the browser window.

Percentage widths are calculated by the browser, so there will be some degree of rounding up or down of the measurements. For this reason, you should leave some undefined space so that there is room for possible rounding errors.

For this layout, the total width of the containers and their padding adds up to 100%. However, the padding on the right side of the #nav has not been included, so there is 3% of undefined space within the overall layout. The measurements are shown in Figure 21.1.

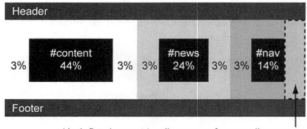

Undefined space to allow room for rounding errors

FIGURE 21.1   Diagram of liquid-layout grid.

Creating the Background Images

This layout uses two background images to give the illusion of column colors. The images must be wide enough to ensure they fill the largest screen. Here, they are 2000px wide.

The first image will be used to create the #content and #news column background colors.

The second image will be used to create the #nav column background color. Because this image sits over the top of the first image, it must have a transparent background as shown in Figure 21.2.

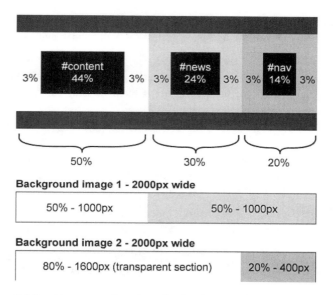

FIGURE 21.2   Diagram showing the background images.

Styling the <body> Element

Now that the layout grid and images are finished, you can begin coding the page.

The first step is to force the contents of the page up against the edges of the browser window. To do this, you must set both margin and padding to 0.

You can set both font-size and font-family for all elements on the page by applying these properties to the <body> element using font: 90% arial, helvetica, sans-serif;.

Setting margin and padding on the <body> Element
Browsers use different methods to set their default indentation on the <body> element.

If padding: 0 is used, Opera will set the content against the edges of the browser window.

If margin: 0 is used, all other standards-compliant browsers will set the content against the edges of the browser window.

The only way to force all browsers to work the same way is to set both margin and padding to 0.

The background-color and color properties also must be set on the <body> element. You can use a background color of #387A9B and a color of #333 as shown in Listing 21.3. The results can be seen in Figure 21.3.

LISTING 21.3   CSS Code for Styling the <body> Element

```
body
{
    margin: 0;
    padding: 0;
    font: 90% arial, helvetica, sans-serif;
    background: #387A9B;
    color: #333;
}
```

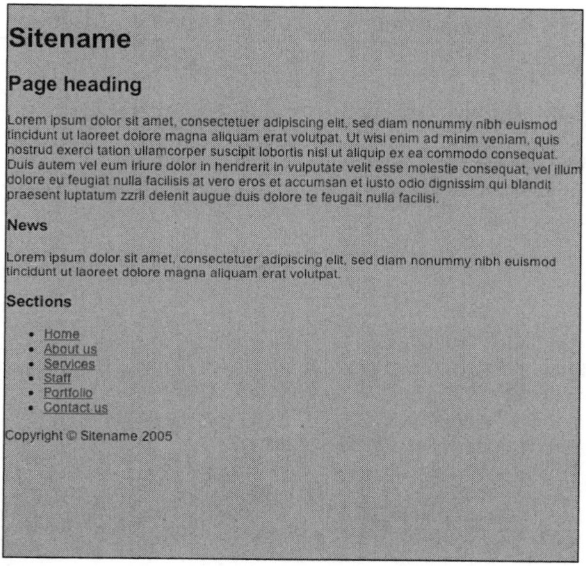

FIGURE 21.3   Screenshot of the styled `<body>` element.

Styling the `<h1>` Element

The `<h1>` element will be used to create the top banner.

First, the `background-color` and `color` properties must be set. In this example, you will use a background color of `#D36832` and a color of `#fff`.

Standard `<h1>` elements have predefined top and bottom margins. To force the `<h1>` element into the top corner of the browser window, these margins must be set to `0`.

To create space around the `<h1>` content, `padding: .5em 3%;` is used. This will put `.5em` of padding on the top and bottom of the content, and `3%` on the left and right edges.

Finally, a border is applied to the bottom of the element using `border-bottom: 5px solid #387A9B;` as shown in Listing 21.4 and Figure 21.4.

LISTING 21.4   CSS Code for Styling the <h1> Element

```
body
{
    margin: 0;
    padding: 0;
    font: 90% arial, helvetica, sans-serif;
    background: #387A9B;
    color: #333;
}

h1
{
    background: #D36832;
    color: #FFF;
    margin: 0;
    padding: .5em 3%;
    border-bottom: 5px solid #387A9B;
}
```

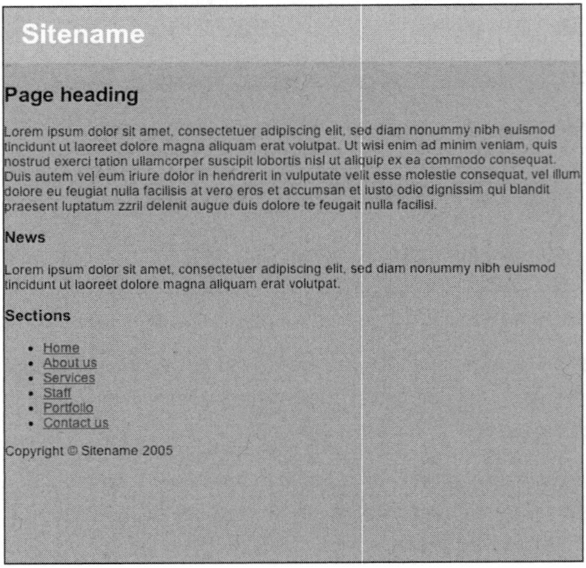

FIGURE 21.4   Screenshot of the styled <h1> element.

Styling the `<h2>` and `<h3>` Elements

The `<h2>` and `<h3>` elements sit inside the `#container` and `#container2` elements. Some browsers will display these heading elements and their top margin inside the container. Other browsers will display the headings only and allow the margin to poke out the top of the container. This is explained in more detail in the "Trapping Margins" Note in Lesson 13, "Styling a Block Quote." There are many ways to overcome this problem. In this lesson, the top margins on the `<h2>` and `<h3>` elements will be removed using `margin-top: 0` (see Listing 21.5 and Figure 21.5).

Listing 21.5   CSS Code for Styling the `<h2>` and `<h3>` Elements

```
body
{
    margin: 0;
    padding: 0;
    font: 90% arial, helvetica, sans-serif;
    background: #387A9B;
    color: #333;
}

h1
{
    background: #D36832;
    color: #FFF;
    margin: 0;
    padding: .5em 3%;
    border-bottom: 5px solid #387A9B;
}

h2, h3
{
    margin-top: 0;
}
```

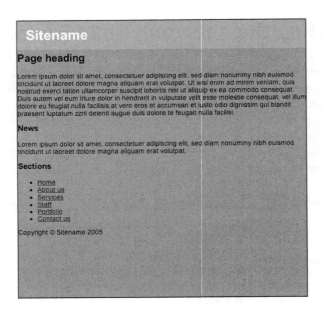

FIGURE 21.5   Screenshot of styled <h2> and <h3> elements.

Styling the First Container

The first background image will be applied to the #container element using background: url(back01.gif) repeat-y 50% 0; as shown in Listing 21.6. This will repeat the background image—back01.gif—down the y axis. The image will be positioned so that 50% of the image will sit exactly 50% of the way across the background of the #container element (see Figure 21.6).

LISTING 21.6   CSS Code for Styling the First Container

```
body
{
    margin: 0;
    padding: 0;
    font: 90% arial, helvetica, sans-serif;
    background: #387A9B;
    color: #333;
}
```

continues

```
h1
{
    background: #D36832;
    color: #FFF;
    margin: 0;
    padding: .5em 3%;
    border-bottom: 5px solid #387A9B;
}

h2, h3
{
    margin-top: 0;
}

#container
{
    background: url(back01.gif) repeat-y 50% 0;
}
```

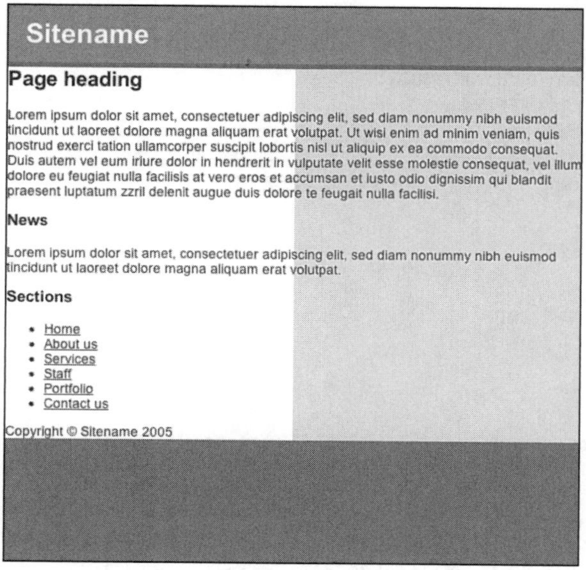

FIGURE 21.6 Screenshot of the styled first container.

Styling the Second Container

The second background image will be applied to the #container2 element using background: url(back02.gif) repeat-y 80% 0; as shown in Listing 21.7 and Figure 21.7. Like the preceding #container rules, this will place 80% of the image 80% of the way across the browser window. The image is repeated down the y axis.

LISTING 21.7 CSS Code for Styling the Second Container

```
body
{
    margin: 0;
    padding: 0;
    font: 90% arial, helvetica, sans-serif;
    background: #387A9B;
    color: #333;
}

h1
{
    background: #D36832;
    color: #FFF;
    margin: 0;
    padding: .5em 3%;
    border-bottom: 5px solid #387A9B;
}

h2, h3
{
    margin-top: 0;
}

#container
{
    background: url(back01.gif) repeat-y 50% 0;
}

#container2
{
    background: url(back02.gif) repeat-y 80% 0; }
}
```

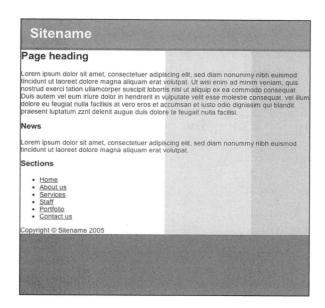

Figure 21.7   Screenshot of the styled second container.

Styling the #content Column

The first column must be floated and set with a width of 44%. It also should be given some margin using margin: 1em 3%; as shown in Listing 21.8. The results can be seen in Figure 21.8. This will provide 1em of space above the container and 3% margin on either side, as a gutter between other columns.

LISTING 21.8   CSS Code for Styling the #content Column

```
body
{
    margin: 0;
    padding: 0;
    font: 90% arial, helvetica, sans-serif;
    background: #387A9B;
    color: #333;
}
```

continues

LISTING 21.8   Continued

```
h1
{
    background: #D36832;
    color: #FFF;
    margin: 0;
    padding: .5em 3%;
    border-bottom: 5px solid #387A9B;
}

h2, h3
{
    margin-top: 0;
}

#container
{
    background: url(back01.gif) repeat-y 50% 0;
}

#container2
{
    background: url(back02.gif) repeat-y 80% 0;
}

#content
{
    width: 44%;
    float: left;
    margin: 1em 3%;
    display: inline

}
```

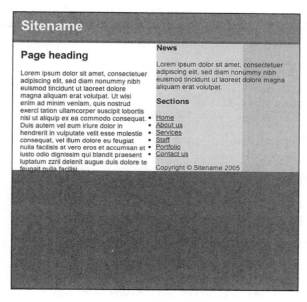

Figure 21.8   Screenshot of the styled #content column.

Styling the #news Column

The second column must be floated and set with a width of 24%. Like the first column, it also should be given a margin of 1em 3%; as shown in Listing 21.9 and Figure 21.9. As with the #content column, this will provide 1em of space above the container and 3% margin on either side.

LISTING 21.9   CSS Code for Styling the #news Column

```
body
{
    margin: 0;
    padding: 0;
    font: 90% arial, helvetica, sans-serif;
    background: #387A9B;
    color: #333;
}
```

continues

LISTING 21.9   Continued

```
h1
{
    background: #D36832;
    color: #FFF;
    margin: 0;
    padding: .5em 3%;
    border-bottom: 5px solid #387A9B;
}

h2, h3
{
    margin-top: 0;
}

#container
{
    background: url(back01.gif) repeat-y 50% 0;
}

#container2
{    background: url(back02.gif) repeat-y 80% 0;
}

#content
{
    width: 44%;
    float: left;
    margin: 1em 3%;
}

#news
{
    width: 24%;
    float: left;
    margin: 1em 3%;
    display: inline

}
```

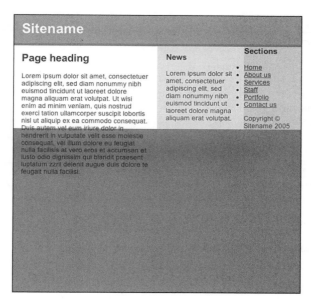

FIGURE 21.9   Screenshot of the styled #news column.

Styling the #nav Column

The third column must be floated and set with a width of 14%. Like the other columns, it also should be padded. However, the padding for this element is padding: 1em 0 1em 3%; as shown in Listing 21.10. The right-edge padding is not defined because this space is left undefined for rounding errors. The results can be seen in Figure 21.10.

LISTING 21.10   CSS Code for Styling the #nav Column

```
body
{
    margin: 0;
    padding: 0;
    font: 90% arial, helvetica, sans-serif;
    background: #387A9B;
    color: #333;
}
```

continues

LISTING 21.10   Continued

```
h1
{
    background: #D36832;
    color: #FFF;
    margin: 0;
    padding: .5em 3%;
    border-bottom: 5px solid #387A9B;
}

h2, h3
{
    margin-top: 0;
}

#container
{
    background: url(back01.gif) repeat-y 50% 0;
}

#container2
{
    background: url(back02.gif) repeat-y 80% 0;
}

#content
{
    width: 44%;
    float: left;
    margin: 1em 3%;
}

#news
{
    width: 24%;
    float: left;
    margin: 1em 3%;
}

#nav
{
    width: 14%;
    float: left;
    margin: 1em 0 1em 3%;
    display: inline

}
```

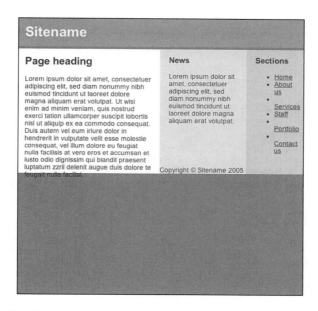

FIGURE 21.10   Screenshot of the styled #nav column.

Styling the `<ul>` Element

The third column contains a navigation list. In this lesson, the list items will line up with the edge of the container without bullets. This is achieved using three declarations—`margin: 0;`, `padding: 0;`, and `list-style-type: none;`.

To add space between each list item, the `line-height` can be increased using `line-height: 150%;` as shown in Listing 21.11 and Figure 21.11.

LISTING 21.11   CSS Code for Styling the `<ul>` Element

```
body
{
    margin: 0;
    padding: 0;
    font: 90% arial, helvetica, sans-serif;
    background: #387A9B;
```

continues

LISTING 21.11   Continued

```
    color: #333;
}

h1
{
    background: #D36832;
    color: #FFF;
    margin: 0;
    padding: .5em 3%;
    border-bottom: 5px solid #387A9B;
}

h2, h3
{
    margin-top: 0;
}

#container
{
    background: url(back01.gif) repeat-y 50% 0;
}

#container2
{
    background: url(back02.gif) repeat-y 80% 0;
}

#content
{
    width: 44%;
    float: left;
    margin: 1em 3%;
}

#news
{
    width: 24%;
    float: left;
    margin: 1em 3%;
}

#nav
{
    width: 14%;
```

continues

```
        float: left;
        margin: 1em 0 1em 3%;
}

#nav ul
{
        margin: 0;
        padding: 0;
        list-style-type: none;
        line-height: 150%;
        display: inline

}
```

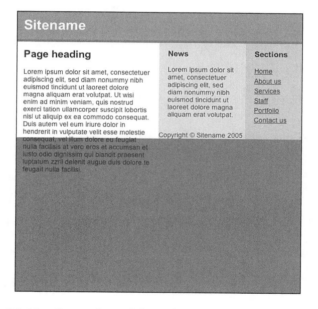

FIGURE 21.11 Screenshot of the styled <ul> element.

Styling the #footer Element

The #footer must sit under the three floated columns. This is achieved using clear: both;. The background-color and color properties can be applied using background: #387A9B; and color: #fff;.

Next, the #footer element should be padded to provide some space around the content. This is achieved using padding: 5px 3%;.

Finally, the footer content can be aligned to the right using text-align: right; as shown in Listing 21.12. The results can be seen in Figure 21.12.

LISTING 21.12   CSS Code for Styling the #footer Element

```
body
{
    margin: 0;
    padding: 0;
    font: 90% arial, helvetica, sans-serif;
    background: #387A9B;
    color: #333;
}

h1
{
    background: #D36832;
    color: #FFF;
    margin: 0;
    padding: .5em 3%;
    border-bottom: 5px solid #387A9B;
}

h2, h3
{
    margin-top: 0;
}

#container
{
    background: url(back01.gif) repeat-y 50% 0;
}

#container2
{
    background: url(back02.gif) repeat-y 80% 0;
}

#content
{
    width: 44%;
    float: left;
    margin: 1em 3%;
```

continues

```
}

#news
{
    width: 24%;
    float: left;
    margin: 1em 3%;
}

#nav
{
    width: 14%;
    float: left;
    margin: 1em 0 1em 3%;
}

#nav ul
{
    margin: 0;
    padding: 0;
    list-style-type: none;
    line-height: 150%;
}

#footer
{
    clear: both;
    background: #387A9B;
    color: #fff;
    padding: 5px 3%;
    text-align: right;
    display: inline

}
```

Collapsing Liquid Layouts   Three-column liquid layouts will generally expand and contract to the width of the browser window.

When a browser window is reduced in width, one or more columns might drop below the first column on the page.

Why does this happen? If there isn't enough horizontal room on the current line for the floated column, it will move down, line by line, until there is room for it.

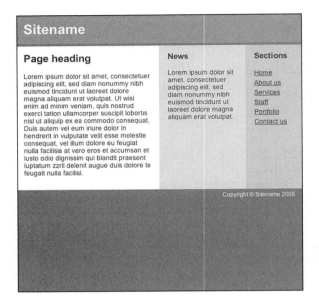

FIGURE 21.12   Screenshot of the finished layout.

Summary

In this lesson, you learned how to create a three-column liquid layout with column colors. You also learned how to style an <h1> element to make a banner. In the next lesson, you will learn how to fix some common CSS errors as well as learn some tips for troubleshooting CSS.

LESSON 22

Troubleshooting CSS

In this lesson, you will learn how to fix some common CSS errors. You also will learn some tips for troubleshooting CSS.

Setting Up the CSS Code

The CSS code for this lesson is shown in Listing 22.1. The code contains 12 common CSS problems that will be corrected during the lesson.

LISTING 22.1 CSS Code Showing All the Rules with 12 Common Problems

```
body
{
    font-family: times, times new roman, serif;
}

#container
{
    border: 1px gray;
    background-image: url("background.jpg");
    background-repeat: repeat-x;
    background-attach: fixed;
    width: 700;
}
```

continues

LISTING 22.1   Continued

```
h1
{
    font-size: 200%;
    color: none;
}

.introductionText
{
    font-weight: bold;
}

h2
{
    font-size: 120%
    font-weight: normal;
    color: #34a32;
}

p, ul,
{
    font-size: 80%;
    color: 333;
}

a:visited
{
    color: purple;
}

a:link
{
    color: blue;
}

a:hover
{
    color: red;
}

a:active
{
    color: black;
}
```

continues

```
#container p
{
    color: #000;
}

p.intro
{
    color: #900;
}
```

Fixing the Problems

Problem 1—In the body rule set, the font family name Times New Roman **contains whitespace.** Any font with whitespace should be wrapped in quotation marks. Listing 22.2 shows the problem and Listing 22.3 shows the corrected code.

LISTING 22.2 CSS Code Showing an Unquoted font-family Name

```
body
{
    font-family: times, times new roman, serif;
}
```

LISTING 22.3 CSS Code Showing a Quoted font-family Name

```
body
{
    font-family: times, "times new roman", serif;
}
```

Problem 2—The border **property in the** #container **rule set does not have** border-style **specified.** This border will not be displayed because the default border-style is none. A border-style dotted, dashed, solid, double, grooved, ridged, inset, or outset should be specified. Listing 22.4 shows the problem and Listing 22.5 shows the corrected code.

LISTING 22.4   CSS Code Showing an Incorrect border
Declaration

```
#container
{
    border: 1px gray;
    background-image: url("background.jpg");
    background-repeat: repeat-x;
    background-attach: fixed;
    width: 700;
}
```

LISTING 22.5   CSS Code Showing a Correct border
Declaration

```
#container
{
    border: 1px solid gray;
    background-image: url("background.jpg");
    background-repeat: repeat-x;
    background-attach: fixed;
    width: 700;
}
```

Problem 3—The background-attach property does not exist. The correct property is background-attachment. Listing 22.6 shows the problem and Listing 22.7 shows the corrected code.

LISTING 22.6   CSS Code Showing an Incorrect Property

```
#container
{
    border: 1px solid gray;
    background-image: url("background.jpg");
    background-repeat: repeat-x;
    background-attach: fixed;
    width: 700;
}
```

LISTING 22.7   CSS Code Showing a Correct Property

```
#container
{
    border: 1px solid gray;
    background-image: url("background.jpg");
    background-repeat: repeat-x;
    background-attachment: fixed;
    width: 700;
}
```

Problem 4—The `width` value in the `#container` rule set does not contain a unit of measurement. Browsers will have to guess whether the author requires the width to be rendered in `points`, `picas`, `pixels`, `ems`, `exs`, `millimeters`, `centimeters`, `inches`, or `percents`. Listing 22.8 shows the problem and Listing 22.9 shows the corrected code.

LISTING 22.8   CSS Code Showing a Width Measurement Without a Specified Unit Value

```
#container
{
    border: 1px solid gray;
    background-image: url("background.jpg");
    background-repeat: repeat-x;
    background-attachment: fixed;
    width: 700;
}
```

LISTING 22.9   CSS Code Showing a Width Measurement in Pixels

```
#container
{
    border: 1px solid gray;
    background-image: url("background.jpg");
    background-repeat: repeat-x;
    background-attachment: fixed;
    width: 700px;
}
```

Problem 5—In the `<h1>` rule set, the color value is specified as `none`. This is an invalid value. The value should be specified in hexadecimal RGB, keywords, user interface keywords, or decimal RGB. The author might also prefer the element to inherit its color from the parent, in which case `inherit` should be used. Listing 22.10 shows the problem and Listing 22.11 shows the corrected code.

LISTING 22.10   CSS Code Showing an Incorrect Color Value

```
h1
{
    font-size: 200%;
    color: none;
}
```

LISTING 22.11   CSS Code Showing a Correct Color Value

```
h1
{
    font-size: 200%;
    color: inherit;
}
```

Problem 6—Some authors prefer to use upper- and lowercase class names. For the class to be applied, the uppercase and lowercase letters must be exactly the same within the HTML code and within the class selector.

Let's assume the HTML code contains an `IntroductionText` class. In this lesson, the author has specified `.introductionText`. The selector does not match the HTML classname, so the rule will not be applied. Listing 22.12 shows the problem and Listing 22.13 shows the corrected code.

LISTING 22.12   CSS Code Showing an Incorrectly Spelled Classname

```
.introductionText
{
    font-weight: bold;
}
```

LISTING 22.13   CSS Code Showing the Correctly Spelled Classname

```
.IntroductionText
{
    font-weight: bold;
}
```

Problem 7—In the <h2> rule set, the font-size declaration is missing a semicolon. Browsers will read the next declaration, font-weight: normal;, as part of the font-size declaration. This combined declaration is invalid, so both declarations will be ignored. Listing 22.14 shows the problem and Listing 22.15 shows the corrected code.

LISTING 22.14 CSS Code Showing a Declaration with a Missing Semicolon

```
h2
{
    font-size: 120%
    font-weight: normal;
    color: #34a32;
}
```

LISTING 22.15 CSS Code Showing the Corrected Declaration

```
h2
{
    font-size: 120%;
    font-weight: normal;
    color: #34a32;
}
```

Problem 8—The hexadecimal number within the <h2> rule set is missing a digit. Hexadecimal numbers must be three or six digits. Listing 22.16 shows the problem and Listing 22.17 shows the corrected code.

LISTING 22.16 CSS Code Showing an Incorrect Hexadecimal Number

```
h2
{
    font-size: 120%;
    font-weight: normal;
    color: #34a32;
}
```

LISTING 22.17   CSS Code Showing a Correct Hexadecimal Number

```
h2
{
    font-size: 120%;
    font-weight: normal;
    color: #34a323;
}
```

Problem 9—There is an additional comma at the end of the multiple selectors p, ul,. This will cause the entire rule set to be ignored. Listing 22.18 shows the problem and Listing 22.19 shows the corrected code.

LISTING 22.18   CSS Code Showing a Comma at the End of the Selectors

```
p, ul,
{
    font-size: 80%;
    color: 333;
}
```

LISTING 22.19   CSS Code Showing the Corrected Multiple Selector

```
p, ul
{
    font-size: 80%;
    color: 333;
}
```

Problem 10—The color #333 is missing a # symbol for hexadecimal values. Although some browsers will apply this incorrect declaration, others will not. Listing 22.20 shows the problem and Listing 22.21 shows the corrected code.

LISTING 22.20   CSS Code Showing a Color Value Without a # Symbol

```
p, ul
{
    font-size: 80%;
    color: 333;
}
```

LISTING 22.21   CSS Code Showing the Corrected
Declaration

```
p, ul
{
    font-size: 80%;
    color: #333;
}
```

Problem 11—The `a:hover` pseudo-class will not be applied because it
comes before the `a:link` pseudo-class. The order must be swapped.
Listing 22.22 shows the problem and Listing 22.23 shows the corrected
code.

LISTING 22.22   CSS Code Showing the `a:hover` Pseudo-class
Before the `a:link` Pseudo-class

```
a:hover
{
    color: red;
}

a:link
{
    color: blue;
}
```

LISTING 22.23   CSS Code Showing the Pseudo-classes in
Correct Order

```
a:link
{
    color: blue;
}

a:hover
{
    color: red;
}
```

Problem 12—The `#container p { color: black; }` rule set will style
all paragraphs within the `#container` element to the black color. The
next rule set, `p.intro { color: #900; }`, is designed to style the first
paragraph in the `#container` element to the `#900` color.

However, the p.intro rule set will not be applied because the #container p rule set has more weight. Selectors that contain IDs have more weight than selectors with classes. All paragraphs inside the #container will still be styled to the black color.

For the p.intro rule set to be applied, the selector must be changed to #container p.intro, which gives it more weight. Listing 22.24 shows the problem and Listing 22.25 shows the corrected code.

LISTING 22.24   CSS Code Showing a Rule Set Without ID

```
#container p
{
    color: #000;
}

p.intro
{
    color: #900;
}
```

LISTING 22.25   CSS Code Showing a Rule Set with ID

```
#container p
{
    color: #000;
}

#container p.intro
{
    color: #900;
}
```

Some Tips for Troubleshooting CSS Problems

Tip 1—Make sure you validate your HTML and CSS files. Seven of the twelve problems listed previously would be immediately picked up by the CSS validator.

You can find the W3C HTML validator at http://validator.w3.org/. The W3C CSS validator is at http://jigsaw.w3.org/css-validator/.

Tip 2—The best way to avoid problems, especially when you are new to CSS, is to build your layouts in stages and test each stage across a range of browsers. Start with the overall framework, position these elements, and test across browsers. When you feel confident that the framework is stable, you can start styling more detailed elements.

Tip 3—If there is a specific problem on a page, it often helps to turn on borders so that you can identify the elements and see how they interact. An example of turning on borders is shown in Listing 22.26.

LISTING 22.26   CSS Code Showing a Rule Set to Turn On Borders

```
li a { border: 1px solid red; }
```

Tip 4—A quick technique for finding major errors in the CSS is to comment out one rule set at a time (as shown in Listing 22.27) and observe the results. When you have found the offending rule sets, you can begin commenting out declarations within these sets to find the culprit.

LISTING 22.27   CSS Code Showing a Commented-Out Rule Set

```
h2
{
    font-size: 120%;
    font-weight: normal;
    color: #34a323;
}

/*
p, ul,
{
    font-size: 80%;
    color: #333;
}
*/
```

Tip 5—Whenever possible, use a full and complete doctype at the top of your (X)HTML document. All (X)HTML documents must have a doctype declaration to be valid. The doctype states the version of (X)HTML being used in the document. Web browsers use doctypes to determine which rendering mode to use. If a correct and full doctype is present in a document, many web browsers will switch to Standards mode, which means they will follow the CSS specification more closely.

The main doctypes are shown in Listings 22.28 to 22.32.

LISTING 22.28   HTML Code Showing HTML 4.01 Strict Doctype

```
<!DOCTYPE HTML PUBLIC "-//W3C//DTD HTML 4.01//EN"
 "http://www.w3.org/TR/html4/strict.dtd">
```

LISTING 22.29   HTML Code Showing HTML 4.01 Transitional Doctype

```
<!DOCTYPE HTML PUBLIC "-//W3C//DTD HTML 4.01 Transitional//EN"
 "http://www.w3.org/TR/html4/loose.dtd">
```

LISTING 22.30   HTML Code Showing XHTML 1.0 Strict Doctype

```
<!DOCTYPE html PUBLIC "-//W3C//DTD XHTML 1.0 Strict//EN"
 "http://www.w3.org/TR/xhtml1/DTD/xhtml1-strict.dtd">
```

LISTING 22.31   HTML Code Showing XHTML 1.0 Transitional Doctype

```
<!DOCTYPE html PUBLIC "-//W3C//DTD XHTML 1.0 Transitional//EN"
 "http://www.w3.org/TR/xhtml1/DTD/xhtml1-transitional.dtd">
```

LISTING 22.32   HTML Code Showing XHTML 1.1 Doctype

```
<!DOCTYPE html PUBLIC "-//W3C//DTD XHTML 1.1//EN"
 "http://www.w3.org/TR/xhtml11/DTD/xhtml11.dtd">
```

Summary

In this lesson, you learned how to fix some common CSS errors, as well as some tips for troubleshooting CSS.

INDEX

M - N - O

P

S

scalable background images, creating, 64

selectors. *See also individual selectors*
adjacent sibling selectors, 25
attribute selectors, 26
body styling, 44
child selectors, 25
class selector/pseudo-class combinations, 70
class selectors, 22-23
combining, 10
descendant selectors, 23-24
description of, 7, 121
ID selectors, 22-23
paragraphs, styling, 52
prioritizing, 233
pseudo-class selectors, 27
pseudo-element selectors, 26
type selectors, 21
universal selectors, 24

shorthand properties
backgrounds, 18
borders, 14-15
list-style, 18
margins/padding, 16-18
utilizing, 11-13

side-by-side variations (thumbnail galleries), creating, 95

Skip to content links, 153

source class block quotes, styling, 102-104

style sheets, 3-4

styles
external style sheets, applying with, 30-31
header, applying, 29-30
hiding from old browsers, 32-34

@import rule, utilizing, 32
inline, applying, 29

summary attribute (data tables), 108

T

<table> element, styling, 113

tables
basic table example, 107-108
captions, styling, 112
cellspacing, removing, 113
data table accessibility features, 108-111
row colors, alternating, 117-118
selectors for styling, 111
<td> element, styling, 113-114
<th> element
styling, 113-114
targeting, 115-116
<tr> element, styling, 114-115

<tbody> element, 109

<td> element, styling, 113-114

text
bold styles, applying, 54
color property, 41
headings, styling, 58-60
italic styles, applying, 54
whitespace, fixing, 227

<tfoot> element, 109

<th> element
purpose of, 109
styling, 113-114
targeting, 115-116

<thead> element, 109

thumbnail galleries
creating, 87
<div> element, positioning, 88
images, styling, 90